By: M. E. Nesser and Brian Robbins

ISBN: 1517262194
ISBN 13: 9781517262198

TABLE OF CONTENTS

Who the Hell Is ME?

You have never met a heterosexual woman so obsessed with pussies in your life. That's why I'd like to introduce you to a dear friend of mine. Her name is ME. Her full name is Mary Elizabeth, but sometimes her name is a little too Catholic for the kind of language that comes out of her mouth, so we stick with calling her ME most of the time.

So what is so special about this ME woman, and why am I dedicating the introductory chapter of this book to her? Trust me; after I tell you a little about her, you may feel compelled to come to Rochester just to meet her.

It wouldn't surprise me if some people think she has a little manic thing going on now and then, because there are times when the Energizer Bunny wouldn't be able to keep up with her. People have wondered if her intensity is generated with some kind of artificial aid, but, believe me, her energy and spirit are all natural and come from an intense need to be successful and happy, as well as for others to feel good about themselves. I can vouch that her wine drinking doesn't start until her workday is completely over.

For the purpose of this book, I want to talk about what ME does for a living. Her profession is so unique and so quirky that this is actually the third book she has written on the subject. For those of you who have never heard of M. E. Nesser or the beauty salon she owns with her husband, you have got to be wondering not only who the hell she is, but what exactly she does for a living. Believe it or not, she has dedicated her career to waxing pubic hair off men and women. Yeah, that really is a profession. Never saw that one coming, did you?

You see, ME is probably one of the busiest and funniest Brazilian-wax technicians you'll ever have the pleasure of meeting. If you aren't familiar with what a Brazilian wax is, please let me enlighten you. It's the type of bikini wax that removes all of a person's pubic and rectal hair. And the intrigue continues...

ME has an interesting story that I'd like to share with you so that you can get a better idea of where she's coming from and what drives her to work as hard as she does. ME moved to Rochester, New York, in 1984, to attend the University of Rochester. Shortly after moving, she met a man named Mark at a local health club. During her senior year, she and Mark got married. ME continued her education by attending Nazareth College, also in Rochester, where she received a master's degree in education.

During ME's stint as an elementary-school teacher, Mark took over his parents' salon. At the time, not only was ME teaching school, but she was also working part time doing artificial nails at the salon, working as a receptionist at Mark's tanning salon, and teaching aerobics. With Mark taking over the business, ME discovered that she had an incredible opportunity to embark on a new career. Mark was an excellent hairdresser and was busy all of the time, so she understood that being a hairdresser could be a fun, successful, and lucrative profession.

Oddly enough, when ME went to beauty school, she realized that cutting people's hair was not her cup of tea. In fact, it made her extremely nervous. It may sound silly, but she always worried about cutting off someone's ear. The ear area can be tricky, especially on someone with short hair, so she kind of panicked when she had to get a scissors near that part of someone's head.

Asian hair also made her nervous, because it is usually so straight. If you don't cut the hair just right, it can look choppy and amateurish. During beauty school, ME would actually go hide in the break room when an Asian client came to the clinic for a cut. Calling her a coward isn't kind, but if the shoe fits...

Bangs were another source of anxiety when she did a haircut. There are way too many women walking around town with bangs that are too short and awkward looking or ridiculously uneven. If you have a funky haircut, then abstract bangs can add to the look. However, most women have fairly sedate cuts that warrant properly cut bangs. And let's not forget the sausage-roll look. We'll never understand that one.

It appeared from the beginning that she was trepidacious following in her husband's footsteps. One thousand hours of beauty school training became very daunting for our girl. So what the hell was she doing in hair school?

When ME took her New York State hands-on licensing exam, she used her poor mom as the model. Believe me, the exam is a long, painstaking afternoon for the models. To top it off, the guinea pigs—I mean models—leave the exam with a less-than-flattering haircut and a lot of gooey crap in their hair.

A few parts of the exam made ME really nervous. For starters, she couldn't seem to wrap a perm rod to save her life. Her fine motor skills disappeared whenever that little end wrap and perm rod were in her hands. The instructors in beauty school stressed how important it was not to drop the rods during the exam. They didn't say anything about shooting them across the room like hand grenades. Another stressful part of the test was the finger waves. I'm not sure finger waves are a trait that most Caucasians are comfortable doing. ME was definitely a white girl during this part of the examination. Her finger waves looked like globs of gel tangled in a cat's hairball.

Although those are only a few examples, you should be getting the picture that, although our girl wanted to be a licensed cosmetologist in New York State so that she could work with her husband, she never had any intention of doing hair. Frankly, she sucked at it. I have to add that her mom said that if ME failed the exam, she would have to find another model for the next time. Nobody blamed her. Lucky for both mother and daughter, ME passed the first time around.

On the other hand, ME certainly never thought that hair removal would be her forte either. Fortunately, she was required to take a waxing class in beauty school. That three-hour class definitively changed her life. The whole concept of playing with Popsicle sticks and hot wax was much more entertaining than she could have imagined. The fact that waxing provided instant results and gratification took that salon service to a whole new level in her mind.

Although she mastered waxing most parts of men's and women's bodies, she wanted to set herself apart and specialize. She always enjoyed being in the spotlight, and here was her chance to do something other's weren't doing yet. She discovered that intimate body part to wax that was unheard of in the early 1990's and ran with it. Ironically, that specialized body part happened to live between women's legs.

As you can probably imagine, she never expected to do Brazilian bikini waxing for a living. I mean, c'mon, who fantasizes about pulling pubic hair out of women's vaginas all day as a potential career choice? She certainly never did. But not only did she find this particular career opportunity amusing, she figured out a way to become really good at it.

She is most definitely good at what she does. In fact, she can comfortably wax women's lady parts every five to ten minutes for nine hours straight without missing a beat. It is unbelievable. She is seriously like Speedy Gonzales doing her thing in the deep, dark bush with a big fat smile on her face. And, boy, does she smile.

She has one of the most positive attitudes of any woman you will ever meet. There is no way anyone is this fucking happy or loves her job this much. But I think she really is and I think she really does. As a matter of fact, I know she is and I know she does.

You probably think that a person who does this all day long would get bored with it. Not ME. She stills gets excited when she sees those big-ass roots on the ends of the pubic hair just lying there, abandoned on the wax strip. She will marvel at a hairy strip like a professional athlete who has just scored the winning goal. And watch out if you have an ingrown hair, because she'll come at you with those scary pointy tweezers, get the look of the devil in her eye, and extract that bad boy like it's the most important thing she does in the entire world.

Her fascination and obsession with pubic hair is something you need to witness to believe. For example, when ME pulls out a pubic hair that is an inch long, you'd think she won the fucking lottery! She gets so excited.

She dances around like a superhero who is celebrating the conquest of her archrival.

I've known ME her whole life, and she has always strived for perfection in everything she does. Her parents gave her a bracelet when she was a teen that read, "Nothing is impossible," and she has tried to live up to that sentiment.

When she did artificial nails for a living, she could hand paint anything on a nail. I've seen her paint the Looney Tunes characters, the Winnie the Pooh Characters, and many other random designs on women's hands. It was impressive for a girl who never took art classes when she was in school. You see, ME went to a private school when she was growing up and always opted out of art classes because she didn't want to get messy. There is so much irony in that, I can't even stand it.

It was fun watching her do nails, but she is so much sassier now that she waxes. Her career has led her to looking at men and women's genital and rectal areas all day long. There is something about this profession that requires a little sass. To think she was worried about getting messy during an art class is way too comical. I think the joke is most definitely on her.

ME comes face-to-face (face-to-pussy, face-to-ass) with some nasty shit during her days, and, for some reason, has gotten over her fear of messes. Actually, I'm not sure if she has gotten over them as much as approaches them as a challenge that she needs to overcome and clean up.

As a random side note (and there will be many in this book), the initials of her name prior to getting married were M. E. S. S. That stands for Mary Elizabeth Suzanne Schaff, in case you wondered. Her initials spelled out the word mess. Isn't that appropriate?

I'm surprised she doesn't continue to prefer being soiled by the acrylic paints she used to use on fingernails then some of the vaginal and fecal matter that she comes in contact with on a daily basis. But I'm not going to discuss anything gross, because our goal in this book is strictly to entertain you.

As ME has grown older, her personality has gotten a lot feistier. I think a lot of it has to do with her husband, Mark. He has a strong personality, and it has made her agreeable nature even sassier. Mark makes some people nervous because he has a loud, booming voice and is intense. But that is why ME is so attracted to him. Intense people tend to be passionate. Everyone could use a little more passion in life, don't you think?

Besides, there has to be something pretty intense going on to keep these two together. They've been together since 1984 and are still able to work and live together after all these years. And I know that being together all the time for so many years would be an impossible feat for most couples, but it seems to work great for these two.

I also know that Mark's strong personality makes ME feel safe. And, in her mind, feeling safe makes her feel even more loved, because he cares enough to always want to protect her. It definitely adds to her commitment and love for him, and I think that's pretty cool.

When ME and Mark first started dating, there were times when his intensity made her uncomfortable. He was so different from anyone she had ever dated before. On one hand, his personality was strong and intimidating. On the other, that intensity was intoxicating and she couldn't get enough. It was funny because one day, someone said something profound that put his personality in perspective. Mark's youngest brother described him in a way that has stayed with her through their thirty-plus-years courtship. Mark's brother told ME that Mark was a "marshmallow with a mouth." Yep, that's a perfect description of her man. She thought it was a strange thing to say about a brother, but it really was the kind of analogy that summed her man up better than anything else she had ever heard.

To know Mark is to love him. He has one of the biggest hearts in the world. What is so endearing about him is that he's the first man to save a wounded animal or hug a crying baby or run to the aid of an elderly person. No man is more aware of his surroundings and more willing to help anyone in need. The funny part of this caring man is that he is usually boisterous in his extremely compassionate and altruistic state, which makes him that much more memorable. So you have to give the two a shout-out, not only for their unique personalities, but also for their longevity. Go Mark and ME!

It has been extremely important to both of them to be good role models for their three kids. Their children have had a lot of friends growing up who were forced to live with parents who didn't love, or even like, each other. They had other friends who were carted from one house to another because their folks had split up. In this age of separation and divorce, they hope their children can emulate what a happy marriage can be like and know in their hearts that it is indeed possible. It has been one of their most prized accomplishments, and they pray their children will experience happy marriages in their lifetimes as well.

The two of them were made for each other. Their partnership, professionally and personally, has made the Mark & M. E. Salon a really special place.

Although ME works her ass off, she is completely devoted to her family. She would do anything for them and worries incessantly about their well-being. Even with three grown kids, not a day goes by that she doesn't think about them and pray for their happiness and safety. Her devotion to her family is another strong bond she has with Mark, which is probably why Mark & M. E. Salon has been such a success. They believe in family. They treat their clients like family. And family is everything. It's a pretty cool dynamic that they have created.

ME's personality was strongly influenced by her parents. Her father was a successful insurance salesman who worked out of their home while she was growing up. He was probably one of the nicest men you would ever have had the pleasure of meeting. Talk about a person who was always smiling! He was never rude to anyone. When people were rude to him, he would kill them with kindness and rational discussion. He was quite the talker. He never saw the benefit of being an asshole to an asshole. He continued to be polite and reassuring no matter how badly he may have wanted to choke someone. ME learned that behavior from him. She is always pleasant and professional no matter how horrid a person is being.

ME's mom was also a positive role model. She exuded a constant sense of joy and energy that would have made the author of *The Secret* proud. Her mom is still a huge part of her life. Thankfully, she supports and encourages all of ME's endeavors. ME is so grateful for that. I'm sure celebrating pussies for a living would make most mom's cringe.

Her parents were self-employed and worked together side by side for forty years. They respected one another and treated each other with kindness and love. ME spent a great deal of time working in the insurance business with them during her formative years and learned much from them. Their hard work and fortitude were attributes she was determined to possess and carry with her through adulthood.

Mark's parents worked successfully and happily together in the salon business as well, which is something pretty cool that Mark and ME have in common. They called the salon Style-O-Rama back then, and it very successful for the forty years when they ran it. Mark's dad changed careers to work with his wife, just like ME did to work with her husband. They had a great business and five awesome sons. Mark couldn't have asked for better role models either.

Now that you have a little background about Mark and ME, you have to be wondering who the hell I am. For those of you who read ME's second book, *The Happy Hen House*, you might have figured out who I am. For the rest of you, let me introduce myself. My name is Raul. I am ME's little voice. ME does not have bipolar disorder or schizophrenia. She just happens to listen to that little voice that lives inside all of us. We think everyone has one, but not everyone chooses to listen to it. ME is all about her little voice. I could probably be referred to as her comical alter ego.

So where do I fit in to this whole Catholic girl's vagina-obsessed story? Let me enlighten you. When something obnoxious or offensive happens in the wax room, I mutter all the frustrations that ME is feeling. And when something absurd or hysterical happens, I only add to her amusement. But I can't restrain myself as well as she can. If someone has dingle berries tangled in their rectal hair, I'm going to have an opinion. If someone's balls smell like last week's trash, I'm going to have an opinion. And if I ever smell fish during a service on a woman, you know that I am seriously going to have an opinion.

But that is who I am. I am ME's little voice who allows her to vent her frustrations and jubilations. I am the side of her that gets frustrated, annoyed, disgusted, and, of course, amused. I protect her from being unprofessional. There have been countless times when she has wanted to say aloud what I was chanting in her head, but she never would. She is just too nice. At least she tries to be. You need to remember that she is the happy chick who writes the happy books and finds happy qualities about every person she meets. It's actually kind of annoying at times. But since I live in her head, I have to feel the love for her.

When we were thinking about writing a third and final happy book (yes, we know you're sad it's the last one), we wanted to make it different. So this is one of the big differences. I'm not letting ME write the book. I'm writing it. Face it; I'm funnier and more honest with my feelings than she is, so I figured it would make our story much more fun this way. I'd hate for our readers to be bored with simply more inane chatter about the cha-cha.

Another way this book is different from the first two is that ME contributed poetry. Writing poetry was cathartic for her during high school and college, so she decided to start writing it again. The only difference, and it is a big one, is that her poems contain different subject matter. Her raunchy rhymes and pussy poems are scattered throughout the book, and we hope you find them amusing. They were definitely a lot of fun to write. If you aren't a fan of poetry, give them a chance. The subject matter and bizarre rhyming in some of them is guaranteed to make you laugh. She has opinions on Adam and Eve, bleeding scrotums, pierced pussies, and even uncircumcised penises.

No matter how you feel about ME as a person, you must admire her tenacity about her profession. She has perfected the art of Brazilian waxing with her skill and humor. She has made tens of thousands of men and women fall in love with her while she puts hot wax on their most private parts and rips it off with the ferocity of a feral animal.

And now we present another book about her hysterical experiences in the wax room. She thoroughly believed in *The Happy Hoo-Ha*, which was the name of the first book of funny stories about her profession that she wrote. In fact, she wishes everyone had a happy hoo-ha, so it's a fitting title. In a way, it has become her mantra. She had a ball writing *The Happy Hen House*, her second book, especially because she let everyone know that it is where every cock wants to go. And now we want to finish off her *Happy Trail*-o-gy with more stories about her journey through the Brazilian rainforest, since she is starting to see an end to this adventure. She hopes that each and every one of you has a positive experience while you travel through *The Happy Trail.*

A Doctor of Her Trade?

Men and women who go into the beauty industry tend to be mentally and physically creative. A good, imaginative brain can lead to beautiful hairstyles, stunning makeup, and intricate nail designs. When creative people are able to put their ideas to work, there are no boundaries to what they can achieve.

When ME was growing up, she liked to dance and play the piano, which are both creative disciplines, but she never really saw herself as a super creative individual. When she started doing hand-painted nail art, she practiced for hours on end to hone her craft until she could draw just about anything a woman would want on her fingernails. And, boy, did her clients want some weird shit painted on their nails!

ME had always enjoyed learning new skills, but that was one that took a lot of effort and time. It was both fun and frustrating. By the time she was ready to give up doing nails, she could hand paint practically anything on a nail.

It wasn't only the adult clients that enjoyed nail art. Little girls wanted hand-painted designs on their nails as well. ME had to learn how to paint Hello Kitty and Dora the Explorer, for example. It was much trickier painting girls nails since, in most cases, the surface area was so much smaller.

She spent a few seasons painting the logos of professional sports teams on avid fans. One football season, for example, she painted a Minnesota Viking head on one of her nails when she and Mark were going to Minnesota to see the Vikings play against Green Bay. It was becoming an amusing skill to have.

Painting on nails was a lot more fun than actually doing the acrylic thing. The application of acrylic nails was fairly tedious and the filing was tough on ME's hands and arms. The nail art, on the other hand, was a blast to do. Back in the late 1980s and early 1990s, women all over Rochester were sporting some pretty creative designs on their fingernails.

Although ME doesn't miss the application of the acrylic nails, she misses the nail art. It was a neat creative outlet for her that brought her a lot of satisfaction. She also misses the time she spent with her nail clients. Doing someone's nails for forty-five minutes every two weeks allowed her to establish an intimate rapport with her clients. She misses that.

When she started writing, she discovered a similar fulfillment as she did doing nails. It has been a great outlet for her. Writing books, blog posts, and poems have been a lot of fun, and she is psyched that people out there are actually reading what she has to say. Being creative with words can be a lot of fun, and you never know what strange and random thing may come out of her mouth. For example, she had a client boast about how much more oral sex she was receiving since she started getting Brazilians. The following poem popped into her head after this woman told her that her boyfriend preferred something more creative than nachos and cheese to eat, so she had to run with it.

Edibles

Twatchos and cheese,
If you please,
Will make you taste better
Than the lint from your sweater,
Wax that beave
So you don't use your sleeve
To wipe off the hair
From her derriere.

Although ME doesn't spend as much time with each individual client anymore, she still enjoys the connections that she makes in the confines of her wax rooms. Obviously, it's impossible not to get intimate with a woman when you are waxing her vagina, unless you're the kind of technician who doesn't talk. And what fun would that be? It's the conversations that make any salon service so memorable. Chicks talk about everything, and I mean absolutely everything. But the conversations that occur while you're waxing someone's most intimate areas take the rapport to a whole other level.

Now ME only spends about ten minutes with each client, but it's a pretty intense ten minutes. Although the chatter has to be more efficient due to the time constraints, you'd be surprised by how many deep, dark secrets are disclosed. Efficient conversation can lead to as much smut talk as a forty-five-minute conversation can. Each exchange is still important, and there are thousands of instances where the talk is much more expressive and intimate. I think it's different because the service is so intimate and peculiar and takes place in a private room. Being naked makes people physically exposed, so it's the perfect opportunity to expose their deep, dark secrets we well.

I guess the point of this conversation was to reiterate what a special time doing nails was for ME, and how she will never forget all the women she connected with during that part of her career. She is truly thankful for those memories.

As ME has gotten older, she feels like the creative side of her personality exists more in her brain than in her hands. Her eyes and hands are too old to paint cartoon characters on small surfaces anymore. That doesn't mean she can't still be creative though. She's just found other ways to showcase the different sides of her personality.

She loves making people laugh and telling them stories. Making people laugh while she waxes off their pubes has made her career so much more fulfilling. It provides such an important diversion to the pain she inflicts. She feels like she has truly become an entertainer in the wax rooms, which I guess is another way to showcase her creative side. It's fun to be funny, and waxing pubic hair off is pretty fucking funny!

When ME is having an expressive exchange with a client, she might appear to be acting somewhat cavalier in her approach to her craft. That could not be further from the truth. She always pays strict attention to the part of the body she is working on. Waxing is a serious job, and she faces countless risks every day. Her demeanor may be lighthearted, but her focus on safety is serious. There are countless times when her heart is racing and she is sweating buckets, but she tries to hide her discomfort or worry with idle chatter so the client doesn't get nervous or worry that something is wrong down there.

Waxing has become such a popular and mainstream service that people probably don't even realize there are any risks involved. On the contrary, technicians who wax for a living must pay strict attention to every aspect of their actions. The main reason any technician should be conscientious when waxing a client is that you never know what you might come across in the hair or on the skin, and you can never predict how a person's skin will react when you yank out their hair from the root. ME tells her employees on countless occasions that every rip counts.

Although ME is not a doctor, she gives advice like one and even acts like one sometimes. There have been a few occasions, however, that have warranted her the imaginary distinction she enjoys. That is why this chapter is referred to as "A Doctor of Her Trade?"

She is the kind of person who pays attention to things that are important in her life, and that includes her clients and what she does to them in the wax room. ME's mom still cannot believe that chicks enter the room, take off their pants and hop on the table, ready to go. It really isn't a big deal, but if you've never had it done, it may seem weird.

When ME wants to know more about stuff, she tends to read books on the subject or searches the Internet. For a while, she actually considered getting a doctoral degree in wellness since she has spent so much time studying both Western and Eastern medicine. She has already attained a master's degree in education, so getting a doctorate has always sounded appealing to her. And don't let her kid you, it still does. However, she started writing books and working hard to build up her clientele and got sidetracked. Besides, they had three kids going to college around the same time she was thinking about going back to school, so it would have been painful to think about another college tuition bill. So if she isn't really a doctor, why am I even bothering to write a chapter about this? Well, let me tell you.

Over the years, ME has found some weird shit on people's bodies that were unusual and sometimes unhealthy. So how should she deal with it, you may wonder? It depends. She'd never want to embarrass someone, but she also wouldn't want to hurt someone or put herself at risk either. The thing is, women's bodies are complicated, and sometimes it's tough to see into all of those crazy nooks and crannies. There could be something weird down there that the client isn't even aware of.

What would you do if you saw a growth or an STD? Ignore it? Pretend it wasn't there? Bullshit. It'd be negligent not to mention something that didn't seem healthy on someone's body. That's where her imaginary MD comes in and rears its nosy little head.

Men and women who work in the beauty industry love giving advice, even if it's not related to the service they provide. It's part of their personalities, since they tend to be outgoing and talkative. They can't seem to help themselves. I think a lot of it has to so with all of the talk about such intimate and personal topics. Bartenders aren't even as lucky as beauticians are when it comes to hearing all the juicy details of someone's life.

Over the years, I've heard ME counsel countless men and women about life, work, sex, and relationships. It's not like she's an expert, but she is older than a lot of her clients and really listens to other's problems when they need to share. You'd be surprised how many of her clients have come to her for advice. That's what forming relationships is all about—sharing feelings and opinions. So that's what she does. So many important topics are discussed that it's impossible to not share her thoughts with her clients. Hell, she has even used her fitness background to help women with their bodies. It seems to be a part of her nature to want to help out whenever she can.

When I look back at all her interactions with the public over the years, it doesn't surprise me that should feel compelled to share some of the interesting scenarios she has come across. She probably could have started her own talk show at this point in her career. Here is one of the poems she wrote about being a doctor and the power that the Brazilian wax has to make you feel better.

Call Me Doctor

Call me doctor,
Call me ME,
Give me your bush,
And I'll set your pussy free.

Feel free to scream,
Feel free to shout,
I'll help you with the problems
You're talking about.

Don't hold back;
Just let me in,
I'll make you feel better.
When it's over, you'll grin.

Don't hold your breath
Or cover your eyes,
Being bare
Is the ultimate prize.

Call me doctor,
Call me ME.
I'll make you feel
The best you can be.

If she notices any abnormalities on a person, she tends to ask what it is, as long as it isn't something that might cause her client embarrassment. If that's the case, she has to weigh the options to find the best way to acknowledge that something is weird down there. Sometimes she avoids it and says nothing. However, since most of us can't see every part of our bodies, she'd feel terrible if she noticed something, didn't say anything, and then that person got sick.

This next story blew me away when we found out what eventually happened. The woman was a newcomer to Mark & M. E., so they had never met before. While this woman was getting her Brazilian, ME noticed a funky mole on this lady's outer labia. She asked the client if she knew it was there and if she had ever had it checked out. The woman hadn't noticed it. She said she felt a bump but assumed it was an ingrown hair. It isn't surprising that she didn't see what it was, since it would have been hard to see something that was buried in her dense pubic hair. It was also located on an area that would have been difficult for her to see without a mirror. She asked ME if she thought she should have it checked out.

Although our girl isn't a dermatologist, she's had some pretty big spots of skin cancer removed from her face, so she has done a fair amount of research about what skin cancer can look like. She asked the client if she tanned naked in the 1980s in tanning beds, like most of the ladies in sunless Rochester, New York, did. Although it may or may not have been a cause, it was something that crossed ME's mind. The woman tanned naked in tanning beds all the time back in the day.

The mole was not perfectly round and was kind of tie-dyed in color. The shape and discoloration seemed creepy, so ME suggested she have it looked at. We found out months later that the woman did see a dermatologist after she got her Brazilian, and the mole was indeed cancerous. In fact, it was melanoma. Fortunately, it was stage zero or one, we can't remember, and they were able to remove all of it. She was grateful that ME pointed it out to her.

That encounter totally reinforced ME's conviction that if she ever saw something suspicious between her clients' legs or anywhere else on their bodies, she would say something.

I'd be remiss if I didn't interject that the whole process of getting a Brazilian and removing all of the pubic hair possibly saved this woman's life. The mole was hidden amidst all the hair that lived between her legs. If she hadn't removed all of it, she may not have found it in time, or even found it at all. So for all of you haters out there who don't believe in this Brazilian wax phenomenon, you may have to be a little more open-minded. Spread your mind. Spread your legs. Spread the love, baby!

Spread 'Em

When you spread your parts,
There may be farts,
But that's OK
'Cause it'll make your day.

Things can hide
Deep down inside
That can affect your health
And act all stealth,

So let's be safe
And stop the chafe
By getting bare
And removing that hair.

It could save your life
And eliminate the strife,
'Cause life is good
When you can see your hood!

That was actually the second growth that ME found. She wrote about the other incident in one of her other books, but I thought I'd repeat the story to give you a quick reminder of how important it is to pay attention to your clients.

The first suspicious growth that ME found was the size of a golf ball in the crease of a woman's buttock. I'm not sure she would ever have found it on her own. It was in a pretty weird spot. The only reason ME saw it was because the client's leg was up in the air, and the growth was slightly protruding out of the crease in her ass where it attaches to the top of her thigh. The woman went to the doctor the same week, and they did surgery right away. They actually thought it could be a form of lymphoma and that it could have been dangerous. I'm happy to say that it turned out to be a benign tumor. The woman called to tell us what happened and to thank us for pointing it out to her. She said the weirdest part of the whole experience was explaining to the doctor how the tumor was discovered. For some reason, it embarrassed her to say that a lady waxing her legs found it.

When you wax pubic hair for a living, it's impossible not to become really comfortable with conversation that relates to the genitalia. One day ME got hurt badly at work. When the doctor asked her what kind of incident had caused the herniation of a disc in her neck, she told him that she was waxing a forty-seven-year-old Italian woman's pubic hair. Unfortunately, the lady's pubes were gray and stubborn, and ME couldn't get them out. She tried to pull the hair from different angles which compromised her posture and bam!, she got stabbed in the neck with a big, thick imaginary knife. The doctor stared at her like a deer in the headlights and said nothing. He was probably trying not to show any shock or ask any more detailed questions, but the lack of expression in his face was kind of priceless. He asked how it happened and she told him! It was probably the only time he had heard of an accident that happened in that interesting manner. Her answer was honest and to the point. It really did happen that way.

Recently, a girl came in who had just had knee surgery. Her leg was bandaged from the middle of her thigh to the middle of her calf. ME noticed the girl's leg was swollen, which wasn't surprising since she had the surgery earlier in the week. When ME started waxing, she noticed that the right side of her genitalia was swollen as well. Now that didn't seem right. She told the client that she should probably have it looked at. It was a Saturday, and the client planned to go to one of our cool festivals after she left the salon, so she said she would probably wait until Monday to get it checked out. The swollen bikini area seemed dangerous, so ME begged her not to wait to call a doctor.

About a month later, the came back for her next wax and said that we literally saved her life. Apparently, her mother agreed with ME about not waiting until Monday to get her leg checked out. When she went to the doctor, they found a blood clot that was traveling up her leg into her midsection. It could have been fatal if she had waited a few more days. Thank God she came in to get waxed that day. And thank God ME has a big mouth.

Referring to ME as an MD may be a bit farfetched, but anyone who spends twenty years doing the same job should be knowledgeable about what they are doing and the products they work with. Yes, the pussy is the product in question. We could actually do something with this…I think the whole PhD concept is probably more appropriate for people in the beauty industry, however. Beauticians like to share. They like to talk. They like to think of themselves as psychiatrists sometimes.

Now let me tell you where her imaginary PhD in psychology comes into the play. We at Mark & M. E. are 100 percent completely sold on the various benefits of Brazilian waxing. Feeling confident and sexy are only two of the reasons every women should experience a Brazilian bikini wax at least once in her lifetime. There are even more benefits than that, but we believe those are two pretty damn good reasons.

One day, ME was telling a woman how waxing would enhance her sex life. The client looked at her and said she didn't believe her. She wanted to know how sex could be better since her lips were so stuck together? She was adamant that there was no way a man could ever get in there! She had a good point. At that particular moment, it would have been logistically difficult for a man to find the entrance that was temporary closed for business. We don't want men near that area for a few hours anyways. Once she used a little oil on her lips and got rid of the sticky residue, this particular client was more confident that she'd be able to use it in the near future. When she felt how soft the area was, she said she could see how sex may not only be possible, but potentially better as well.

Women who are uncomfortable about the size or shape of their vaginas often ask us for advice about labiaplasty or labia reduction or reconstruction surgery. As a dude, I personally cannot imagine anyone spending thousands of dollars having plastic surgery on her pussy—but then again, why the fuck not? If I had to choose between a good-looking one or ne that was not so good looking…Honestly, if it was disfigured, I'd say, go for it! I'd probably be looking into getting it done as well. More importantly, I think a woman should do whatever she needs to do in order to feel good about her body. And who would want that part of her anatomy to be weird looking? I mean, a lot of good stuff happens in that area in a woman's lifetime, so why not do whatever it takes to make it as pretty as possible?.

I heard a story that made me understand why this surgery not only could be important to a woman, but even life changing. We met a girl with lips that hung so low, she had to tuck them inside her body so they didn't hang down like a man's testicles. It's hard to imagine, but she said that they hung down so far, they were actually visible through her clothing. I can't imagine how mortifying that would be for a young girl to deal with. She never wanted to wear a bathing suit or fitted clothing. It was embarrassing for her in high school, and especially when she did sports and had to change in the locker room in front of her teammates. She had surgery to trim them down. It changed her life.

This story blew me away. I couldn't imagine having lips droop so low that I'd have to tuck them inside my body. That alone had to feel awkward and uncomfortable. It had to have been so embarrassing if they fell out while this young lady was wearing fitted clothing or a bathing suit. In addition, the idea of changing in a locker room in front of a room full of girls had to be so horrifying for her. I couldn't be happier that she had this problem fixed.

There are so many obscure situations out there that I don't think anyone can judge other people for anything they choose to do to their bodies. In addition, the majority of the population really can't imagine what this girl felt like. It had to be awful. Maybe the idea of labiaplasty isn't as absurd as it may have first seemed.

Another woman came in after her second labia correction surgery to correct her misshapen labia. They put sixty-four stitches in her lips to close them up after they cut some of the excess skin off. (Sixty-nine would have been so much more appropriate of a number.) She still had the stitches in when she came to get waxed. It was nerve wracking to wax around an area that had that so many stitches in it. Who are you kidding? ME was sweating her proverbial balls off! She commented that it looked really freaky with all of the stitches still in the edges of the skin.

The client she called it her FrankenPuss. It was cool that she had such a good sense of humor about it, but it was still nerve wracking to wax around an area with so many stitches still in place, regardless of what she called it. It was scary looking and made ME's pussy ache just thinking about it.

Sex can be amazing when you've had a fresh Brazilian, but women get overanxious about their newfound freedom and want to have sex right away, which is never a good idea. Your skin needs a chance to heal and calm down. There's no exact number of hours before you can have sex, because every person is different. But you need to wait.

I once overheard a woman talking about having sex way too soon after her wax. She said that if you don't wait long enough to have sex after you get a Brazilian, your man's penis will feel like a salty pretzel rod rubbing against an open wound. Now that's an interesting visual. For the record, when women demand an exact time frame, we usually tell them to wait until the next day.

Salty Pretzel Rod

Removing the hair
From your innermost lips
Makes you feel sexy
From your head to your hips.

When you first take off the hair,
It's tender to touch,
And too much friction
Will hurt so much.

You must wait
Many hours or more,
Or you won't be happy
When he goes through your door.

If you don't wait
For him to enter your bod,
His penis will feel
Like a salty pretzel rod.

This past Valentine's Day was absolutely insane at Mark & M. E. It fell on a Saturday, and it was unbelievable how many women came in to get waxed that day. If any of them had asked our opinion, we would have told them to get waxed earlier in the week. But no, about sixty women came into Mark & M. E. to get waxed on February 14, 2015. Some were probably perfectly fine to get lucky later that day, but there were countless others who really shouldn't have gotten down and dirty until the next day. Common sense tends to get clouded when you're horny and the prospect of getting laid is in the immediate future. Moral of the story: women need to plan better and think with their heads instead of what lies beneath their hoods.

What totally surprised us most about that day was all of the newbies who came in. In most cases, the skin gets more pissed off the first time you get a Brazilian. Getting one the day of any celebration isn't smart. Sex clouds the judgment of even the brightest scholars. You think more women would use better common sense when it comes to their pre-sex grooming preparations. Live and learn.

We carry a product called The Happy Hoo-Ha Numbing Cream that helps numb the area before a wax. It contains 4 percent lidocaine and many people find it helpful. Aside from a topical anesthetic and maybe a couple of ibuprofen, we don't recommend that clients take drugs before they come in. Every once in a while, however, someone expresses the desire to be intoxicated with either drugs or alcohol to better deal with the pain.

One day, one of our employees knocked on one of the wax-room doors and asked us if we needed anything. ME said she was good and didn't need anything and thanked her for asking. The client, on the other hand, sat up and screamed, "I need pain-killers!"

As you can see, it can be fun playing doctor. In our profession, our work makes playing doctor that much more satisfying. When you've been doing anything for a long time, you learn more about your trade and that makes it possible to offer more valid advice. If we can be helpful in any way, we're definitely going to try. Real-life experience in any field over the years can give anyone an imaginary MD, PhD, or maybe just an FoS—full of shit, anyone?

Sassysnatch

Keeping up with the ever-changing technology in our society has been interesting for ME. Believe it or not, she received a master's degree without a computer, so doing all this Internet crap has been quite the feat over the past few years. Doesn't that seem hard to imagine that anyone could secure higher-level education without a computer? She used this old-fashioned piece of machinery called a typewriter in graduate school to write all her papers. It was electric, which made it much more sophisticated than the manual ones. She never used a computer for anything. In fact, she didn't even know how to use a computer until she was in her thirties.

If she needed to do research, she went to that pretty building where you take a nap that is really quiet. You know, the library. It was where all her research took place. She looked things up in books. Sounds prehistoric, doesn't it?

Now, she can't go anywhere without her Mac. She buys purses large enough to accommodate her computer. She can't imagine writing any of her "happy" books without one. Shit, her phone is a miniature computer, and she doesn't go anywhere without that either. In fact, she keeps it under our pillow when she sleeps. Don't judge. You'll have teenagers who do stupid shit one day also. It's been important to try to keep up with the changing technology, even if she sometimes feels like an idiot doing it.

ME feels like she needs another degree to make herself more proficient in computers so she can stay on top of all of the technological demands in our society. OK, maybe not on top of the demands, but at least proficient enough to not feel like a total moron. Dealing with the social-media bullshit on a daily basis can be a full-time job. For the past few years, she has been trying to keep up with our Twitter account. She tweets under the name Sassysnatch, and we have to admit it has been a lot of fun. We enjoy tweeting about twats and twat-related things. We're not sure if it's helped our business any. Furthermore, I'm not sure that it's helped sell her books either. However, she has to try to keep up with the current trends, and we never underestimate doing something that's fun.

We cannot figure out this whole hash-tag business either. We do it. We aren't sure why, but it's supposed to be important, so we try to hash-tag a mess of different pussy-related words. Several computer-savvy people have tried to explain this whole hash-tag thing, but it's hard to understand how it works and why it helps. ME puts that little tag symbol in front of random words on a regular basis in hopes that one of the words she wrote down will come up on the list. Some of the words and phrases people tag make absolutely no sense. Some are just flat-out absurd, and maybe that's the point. In any case, she'll keep up with this until someone tells her it's a total waste of time and that there are other avenues where she can channel her creative energies.

ME also writes a blog on a daily basis. I think she has blogging figured out. The copy-and-paste thing from the blog to her Facebook pages is easy and only takes a second. She blogs every morning, and then pastes the post to her two Facebook pages, which are the www.marknme.com web page and ME's personal page, which is just her name Mary Elizabeth Nesser. There's probably some fancy way for the blog to automatically transfer over, but we're not that sophisticated, and we seem to bother our nerdy Apple Genius friend more than we should, so we just stick to the copy-and-paste thingy.

We should take a minute to give a shout-out to our technical savior. His name is Jon Silva. He created both the Mark & M. E. and M. E. Nesser websites. He also keeps us sane when we are losing our minds to all this advanced technological crap we're trying to keep up with. His help has been priceless, and we'll never be able to thank him enough for all his patience and help.

ME's blog is not fancy. It's just a place she goes to write some random shit about pussies on a daily basis. Hell, she's up to over 2,000 blogs. Didn't I tell you she likes to talk? You have to like the name. It's amusing, to say the least. *Hose Down Your Hoo-Ha* has such a nice ring to it. There are times when the title is very poignant as well.

One of the reasons she has remained so diligent with her blog is that she heard of a few blogs that have become blockbuster movies. ME has used the material from her blog to help her write her "happy" books, and she will probably need some divine intervention when it comes to making anything huge out of her work. You never know though, stranger things have happened. In this day of *Fifty Shades*, who wouldn't want a fun series about living in a world full of naked women and naughty stories? So ME will continue spreading her love of the snatch through words until someone, somewhere latches on and takes her for another crazy ride. Showtime, are you listening?

Embracing Lust

Most people love
To listen to lust
Every once in a while.

Girls prefer books,
Dudes prefer porn—
It doesn't matter what the style.

Sex can be great,
Sex can be fun;
It keeps the world alive.

Lust is great,
Lust is fun;
It's how we humans thrive.

Believe in love,
Believe in touch;
It'll make you want to live.

Enjoy your body,
Give in to passion;
You have so much to give.

Remember to listen
To your inner lust
Again and again and again.

And to live life
To the absolute fullest
Until it has to end.

So we were talking about the demands that social media puts on businesses and how we need to decide if we're going to participate in it or just ignore it completely. With all the competition in the beauty industry, it would probably be a lousy business decision to ignore the benefits of engaging in some of the available social-media outlets. That is, if you don't have a nervous breakdown trying to figure all of it out.

So let's talk about Facebook. Ugh. They changed the rules with the business Facebook accounts so that now only a tiny percentage of our followers see our posts every day. We went from roughly one thousand views a day to a little over one hundred. In order to reach more people, we have to pay Facebook to "boost" our page so it gets seen by more people. Is that a crock of shit or what? I know ME would like to tell Facebook to kiss her ass. Oops, I think she just did.

Since Facebook decided to change the rules, ME now posts her blog to her personal Facebook page, because it gets so much more attention. I wouldn't be surprised if some of her followers think she's lost her mind with some of the crazy shit she posts. When a daily post says that she had a good day because nobody passed stinky gas in her face, what would you think? This bitch is bat crazy. That's what I'm thinking your friends would think. Or how about when she boasts that she had a good day because she didn't pull any strings or piercings out?

Speaking of which, check out this poem that tells the painful tale of her of doing just that.

The Pierced Pussy

You never ever know
What you're going to find
When you spread a girl's legs–
You are going in blind!

When I look at the shape
And I look at the size,
I can never predict
If there's a door prize.

But the thing that has probably
Surprised me the most
Is the decorative jewels
So many girls boast:

Some piercings are small,
And some are so shiny;
I'm still waiting to find one
In somebody's hiney!

I have to admit,
I do feel some fear
That I'll rip out the jewels,
And then screams you will hear!

I am so very careful
When applying the wax;
Hair is all I want to remove.
It's so hard to relax.

One fated day
I had wax on my glove,
And the jewel went flying
Like a fast, soaring dove.

The woman was pregnant—
Nine months to be exact—
And I'm relieved to say
Her skin was intact.

Her stretched-out skin,
For what it is worth,
Was soft and pliable
And ready for birth.

The experience that day
Gave me a fright,
And I drank a lot of booze
Deep into the night.

If your pussy is decorated
With silver or with gold,
I'll take extra care
With each and every fold.

But it might be smart
For you to tell me it's there,
So I don't remove anything
But your unwanted pubic hair!

Let me tell you, ME was completely freaked out when the client's piercing flew across the room. In twenty years of waxing and seeing hundreds of piercings, that had never happened. Fortunately, she was able to put it back in and all was good.

That night, ME was still upset about it. She went out to dinner and Mark asked her what she wanted to eat. She said gin. He said, "No, to eat?" She said gin. She told him it was a really stressful day. He said, "Why, because you ripped that chick's piercing out?" She asked him how he knew. He told her that he asked the woman how it went when she came down to cash out. She told him that ME ripped her piercing out and it went flying across the room. He sure had a good time teasing his wife about it.

Three years passed since that dreaded incident occurred. One day, a woman came in for a wax with her three-year-old child. The child sat in the rocking chair in the corner of the room. ME asked the woman if she had ever had a wax before. The lady said that she hadn't had it done in three years since she was nine months pregnant. She told ME that she had gotten her wax at Mark & M. E. and that the woman who waxed her ripped her piercing out and it went flying across the room. ME said, "That was me!" The client didn't recognize her and was able to laugh about it since she hadn't been hurt when it happened. She came back, so it mustn't have been as traumatizing to her as it was to ME. She still sports the same piercing, and there was no harm done. Thank the Lord!

At this point, I think ME would prefer that we get back to our social-media discussion, because she's starting to feel nauseous remembering that dreaded Friday afternoon. Yes, she clearly remembers what day of the week it was. Wouldn't you?

She recently started using her personal Instagram account for business, since that's supposed to be the new cat's meow. We're not really sure how this helps us out with new clients or book sales either, but we get giddy when people "like" our pictures. I guess that accounts for something. Besides, we heard somewhere that Instagram is the most popular way to go these days, so we better do our best to keep up with it. By the time this book gets published, there'll probably be some other social media craze she'll have to master.

ME also has an app called TweetCaster on her phone that she tries to update once in a while. It is a Twitter site that goes directly to the www.marknme.com web page. It's on the front page of the website, and she has been trying to be better about updating its status. Sometimes she forgets to write something new, and the post will read, "Happy Valentine's Day!" on April 7. Although she may not be the most technologically savvy person, you have to give her props for trying to remember all this stuff. From typewriter to Twitter, she's come a long way, baby.

But what her job really comes down to is people. She works on people all day. She interacts with people, physically and emotionally, all day long. One of the reasons she likes to share stories with the public is that her profession is so unique. She goes to the inner sanctums of the human body to accomplish her task, and what she finds never ceases to amaze her.

Into the Inner

Skin...
Everyone is shaped a little differently—
Loose or taut, it doesn't matter.

Semen...
Some women have no etiquette.
It can have such a pungent smell.

Paper...
Guaranteed to make the stomach flip,
It belongs in books, not in creases.

Discharge...
Unpleasant is a kind description.
It can create such a mess.

Crust...
Should be exclusive to pizza—
End of story.

Dingleberries...
Only the word is cute.
There are no words.

Jewelry...
Decorations make me smile;
Accessorizing can be fun.

ME the Cheerleader

Everybody has multiple facets to their personality, but most people have one trait that is more dominant than others. Some people are inherently shy. Others are outgoing. Some have engaging, energetic personalities, while others speak quietly and with no affect. There are dominant and submissive people (who have always intrigued us and whom we love to read about). Not everybody has the need to be in control, but, for some reason, ME does. She can't remember a time when she had the need to be a follower. Having control in the wax room is important. It shows the client that you are confident and not timid about what you're doing. The really cool thing about the job is having the opportunity to interact with such a diverse population throughout the workday and enjoying the divergent personalities that walk through the door of the salon. Diversity makes life so much more fascinating.

ME has always been an outgoing person who is inherently happy and positive. It's just how she is. For as long as she can remember, she has enjoyed facilitating situations in an energetic and enthusiastic way. When I got thinking about how she is when she interacts with the public, I decided that ME reminds me of a cheerleader.

Don't scoff at the comparison. The analogy of a cheerleader doesn't have to be demeaning. In fact, comparing her to a cheerleader, in my mind, is a compliment. I've thought long and hard about how she presents herself to others, and once you see her in action, I think you'll agree that she is most definitely the kind of woman you'd find with a pom-pom in her hand.

Since middle school, ME has loved being on stage. She was the lead in the play *The Ugly Duckling.* That was funny, because they put a clay nose on her to make her look ugly and disfigured, but her real nose was so small that nobody noticed any difference or thought she looked strange. She was Cinderella in a ballet performance when she was in middle school, which was really exciting. She cut her hair off and went to Florida and got pretty tanned right before the debut, which really pissed her ballet instructor off. Ballerinas were supposed to be fair skinned with their hair in nice, neat buns. She couldn't bun her short hair, and she was anything but fair skinned.

In high school, she was in a song-and-dance group called the Triple Trio. Although she didn't have a good singing voice by any means, it was fun and allowed her to be on stage. She also got to dance, which she loved.

NFL cheerleaders perform in front of hundreds of thousands of people. They're on stage. It's just a different kind of stage then a play or ballet. Their stage is full of big, strong, sweaty men, and that sounds pretty fun. Oh how we love to see all of those sweaty men in their tight pants! You have to admit that it's pretty ballsy to get up on a stage and perform before any size audience.

In high school, ME started an aerobics program. She hated sports and had to quit ballet because she had shitty knees. It became so popular that not only were the classes filled to capacity, she received a varsity letter when she graduated. It was a fun and memorable experience because even a few teachers took her classes. A lot of the time, she got out of school early and went to a local bar and drank before the workout. It was the '80s. Things were different back then. It was such a high for ME to yell at her peers while singing, screaming, and getting all crazy to fun, loud music. In order to legitimize the aerobics program, she taught five days a week for ninety minutes every day. Shit, if you think about it, she probably should have asked for some kind of compensation.

A small group of girls actually tried to start a cheerleading squad in high school since ME's boyfriend did three varsity sports and was the captain of the teams. She was going to all of the games anyways, so it seemed like a good idea since her private school didn't have any kind of cheerleading program. As it turned out, it wasn't that good an idea at all. They weren't very organized. They went drinking before the games. They didn't have a lot of cute cheers. Actually, from what ME has told me, they were kind of obnoxious. It didn't go well, and it didn't last very long. She liked making up rhymes and coming up with strange combinations of words and phrases, so I think you can understand what prompted her to try the whole cheerleading gig.

The H *Factor*

Haunting hormones
Hungry heathens
Habitual hard-on
Heavenly hips
Honest hedonism
Hidden hood
Humping horndog
Hair-raising holler
Hearty homerun
Hefty heinie
Head-banging husband
Horrifying hemorrhoids
Horny husbands
Happy happy hoo-ha

She continued to teach aerobics in college because she loved dance, exercise, and music. It seemed like a no-brainer to have a company pay you to work out, and then use the facilities for free. It's painful to pay for a gym membership now, especially since she goes to the most expensive joint in town. I guess that since she is at a more mature age now, she should be able to justify spending the money. Don't think it doesn't make her cringe just a bit. Who are we kidding? She used her tip money from the salon and paid the last few months with fives and tens so it didn't feel as painful to hand over the $160 a month they charge.

She always believed in the motto that "fitness is for life." We aren't sure who coined the phrase, but we like it. ME always loved to dance and to listen to music. Teaching fitness classes was a great outlet for her to share her enthusiasm for all of the above. She loved having control over a class and trying to make them get a kick-ass workout and have a blast while doing it. Honestly, teaching aerobics was one of the most enjoyable things she ever did for work. It never felt like work to her because she loved every minute of it.

Being a schoolteacher also gave her the control to try to offer a positive learning environment for the students. She was organized and creative and tried hard to not make learning a boring and tedious struggle. M.E. tried to make her lessons fun and inspiring, just as she has tried to do in her current profession. She also worked with elementary students, which made it easier to add levity and creativity to the curriculum. Teaching was never really her gig. She didn't love it, and it's always been important for her to love what she was doing. The biggest downside to the whole teaching thing was that she had to follow the school's and New York State's rules, which wasn't the easiest thing for her to do. There's a little rebel living inside this one, you know. She's not an obedient type of woman. She doesn't really like to follow the rules. Maybe that's why she likes doing Brazilians for a living. It's a little naughty and controversial. Believe me, ME definitely likes to be naughty and controversial.

These days, she feels like a cheerleader when she is in the wax rooms. The reality is that waxing can be painful, and it's her job to help clients get through it. She can't have clients get so discouraged that they might lose that all-important game. She focuses on boosting your morale and keeping your spirits up in spite of how you may be feeling, just like a cheerleader. Her goal is to keep you encouraged and never give up until you reach the finish line.

If you think there is time to wait between rips, think again. ME has never been fond of procrastinating over anything in her life, including waxing your pussy. Even in her personal life, she goes crazy when her kids procrastinate. It drives her absolutely nutty. She tends to respond to them as she does her job. Be encouraging and supportive and persevere until you finish.

Even though her kids procrastinate in certain areas of their lives, they are hard workers. Thank Goodness, because Mark & ME would have a melt down if they were lazy asses. They have positive, outgoing personalities like their parents, which is definitely not a surprise. She and Mark are proud to recognize that they have all exhibited leadership qualities in some part of their lives. Whether it was in sports, dance, scholastic, or social situations, all three of them possess a little bit of that cheerleading quality that ME is so fond of. The apples absolutely don't fall far from the Mark & ME tree.

Speaking of apples...Mark's brother has been in advertising for over thirty years. He started in radio, and then progressed to television. We told him we were thinking about advertising on the radio. He said he had come up with a concept to advertise for the salon that he thought would be effective. It was a fifteen-second ad. For the first four seconds, there was jungle music. Then ME said in her most provocative voice, "Hey, big fella, want a bite of my apple?"

Then a man said, "Not until you get a Brazilian at Mark & ME." Then you hear a bite of an apple, ME giggle, and another bite of an apple. It's a really funny ad that most definitely got people's attention. We were actually surprised that the radio station agreed to air the ad. We were so glad they did though. The reaction to the ad was incredible, and it caused a lot of buzz around town. Let's not forget to offer a big shout-out to Mark's brother for having a sassy, creative mind.

It just occurred to me that cheerleaders would be a great group of women for ME to partner with. Who needs a wax more than a bunch of scantily clad girls? Between their short skirts and all that skin showing, they have a huge need to keep themselves well groomed. We would love to tap into that market in more ways than one. Life is full of so many options.

Some of you probably can't be bothered with this whole cheerleader discussion because it is so superficial and degrading. We beg to differ. There may be negative Nellies and haters out there who dismiss cheerleaders simply because they have amazing bodies. C'mon, be honest; since when is having a kick-ass body a bad thing? If a girl is as dumb as a doorknob, then I guess her body would be less alluring and you can be prejudiced against her stupidity. Not for nothing; having a fit, hot body takes a lot of hard work. Even having beautiful hair and makeup takes effort. They don't wake up looking like that. I'd like to suggest we applaud all the diligent effort they take to look amazing instead of criticizing them. Face it, my friends. I doubt you'd be searching for the noose if you looked like that.

Cheer Them On

When the players do their hits,
The girls shake their tits.
When the players go to score,
The girls cheer for more.
When the players get knocked out,
The girls scream and shout.
When the players do their dance,
The girls do a prance.
When the players throw it bad,
The girls act all sad.
When the players throw it good,
The girls know they could.
When the players win the game,
The girls shake it with no shame.

ME asked her son's friends what adjective came to mind when they thought of cheerleaders. One friend said flexible. Yes, they do need to be flexible. I'm sure that flexibility helps prevent injuries and can improve the quality of their work. I also imagine that being flexible provides a variety of benefits outside of their profession and in their personal lives as well. (It was impossible not to turn that into a sexual comment.)

His other friend said voluptuous. From what I've observed, cheerleaders have nice breasts. Even though I am a gay man, I have always admired nice breasts. Whether they have implants, have naturally awesome boobs, or a wearing a kick-ass bra, it doesn't really matter. I do know that they don't look like flat-chested little boys in their skimpy outfits. Gay or straight, you should always admire a nice set of boobs.

ME remembers her dad saying that anything more than a handful (or mouthful, we can't quite remember) was a waste. I think that's a delicate and politically correct comment when you are in love with a woman with smaller titties. I would have to challenge any man who would say, "Oh, I'm sorry, but your full, C-cup boobs are too big to fit in my mouth." I think most men would suck it up (pun intended) and do their best to enjoy the boobs that were presented to them.

The fitting in the hand thing is even more debatable. One man may have small hands like Napoleon. Then a "A" cup would be perfect. What if your guy had hands like Andre the Giant? Everyone's perception of too small or too big is subjective. My contention is that it's hard not to admire a nice rack. OK, that's probably not the classiest thing to say, but neither is this discussion. I also think that, unless the breasts are grotesquely oversized, most men would enjoy them no matter what letter of the alphabet they repesent.

With all of that jumping around and lifting their knees up and down, do you think the cheerleaders are aroused by their lips rubbing together? Just one of those random thoughts that I felt compelled to share. Inquiring minds...All I know is that cheerleaders can't have pubic hair. Their outfits are too damn skimpy and that's OK, because we're all about bald beavers in this house.

Bald Beaver

There is something enchanting about a beaver that's bald,
And it really doesn't matter what it is called.
When the hair disappears and it's in your face,
The impending orgasms can take you to space.

I know a dentist who thinks flossing is good,
But not when you're facing a pussy and some wood.
Your teeth should be cleaned on your own precious time,
Not when you're celebrating with tequila and lime.

Paper and gunk can get trapped in the hair;
Foreign matter is too gross to share.
When the hair is all gone and there is just skin,
You'll do absolutely anything to get right in.

So next time you find a woman who waxes her beave,
Don't even hesitate or try to leave.
Put on your glasses and check it all out;
I know you'll be satisfied, without any doubt.

Provided that our cheerleader isn't a Valley girl or a space cadet, I think we should applaud her enthusiasm and leadership skills. Those traits can be beneficial in life. I know that ME has used them with great success. I'm sure there are still many of you who think that looking like Barbie is condescending and beneath you. Let me ask you this. Who wouldn't want to have a great body and be beautiful? There has to be some part of you, as a woman, that wouldn't mind looking like Barbie. Let's face it, what Ken wouldn't want to fuck a Barbie?

Ripping for a Living

So how does a nice Catholic girl end up ripping pussies for a living? Are nice Catholic girls even supposed to say the word pussy? I think *not*!

There are so many reasons for the career move. For starters, she wanted to work with her husband. It was a natural thing to do, since both sets of parents worked together for forty years each. What's really cool is that Mark's folks were both hairdressers in the current location where Mark and ME currently work. His mom started the salon when she was eighteen years old. It's kind of neat to think that Mark and ME are following in their parents' footsteps. Working with her husband seemed like the right thing for her to do. I think they were destined to work together. And to this day, she never regretted changing careers to work with Mark. It's probably one of the best decisions she made in her life.

It's funny that in 1984, when ME first met Mark, she didn't even know what waxing meant or what it referred to. She had a normal amount of pubic hair, nothing scary, and it never occurred to her to do anything about it. Shit, she vividly remembers the first time Mark suggested she tweeze her eyebrows. She asked him (not so nicely I might add) what was wrong with her eyebrows, because she thought they looked fine. He said they would look better tweezed. She told him if he wanted them tweezed, he'd have to do it. What the hell was she thinking? It fucking hurt! She told him to get away from her face. That was how this whole hair removal thing started.

A lot of things have changed since then. Now she waxes her whole body, as do a lot of people. In addition, pubic hair has virtually become extinct (as has pubic lice), thanks to people like ME who take off thousands of women's pubic hair every year. We got thinking about what it's like in today's world when you go on a first date and this is what we came up with.

First Date

You go on a date,
And what do you find?
A big hairy bush
That could render you blind.

So what do you say
When you see this big mess?
Oh, excuse me,
But does a bird live in your nest?

She goes down on you
And finishes the job,
So now it's your turn
To try to find her nob.

I hate to say it but
Hesitation is not your friend,
It makes her feel unwanted,
And she'll want it to end.

So what is the plan
When you come across hair?
Picking pubes out of your teeth
Is not fun to share.

Maybe a talk
Should happen prior to the date:

Are you sporting a big bush,
Or do you like to clean your plate?

In this day and age,
People know what they want.
We need an emoji
Designed in a cool
New font.

It would express our preference
For the bush down below,
So there'll be no surprises,
And you'll know who to blow.

You have to wonder why else ME decided to rip people's hair out for a living. The second reason is that she makes a decent living. It was important to both of them to provide a good life for their children, and they have done just that. Education and hard work are important to them, and they tried to instill that work ethic in their kids. If you're willing to put in the time and education and have some talent, being a beautician is a pretty awesome gig.

Random people have criticized them over the years for the nice cars they've driven and the vacations they've taken. You will never hear them apologize for finding some success in their lives, because they have worked their asses off to provide a good life for themselves and their kids. Jealousy is ugly. Besides, owning a salon is not the only thing they do. They currently own rental properties in New York and Florida, which supplements their income. That also takes a lot of time and hard work. They are proud of how hard they work, and their efforts have definitely paid off.

Mark and ME are both college educated, which actually separates them from a lot of people in this industry. It has really helped with the success of their business and is one of the reasons they insisted that their children all go to college. To this day, they continue to work on a lot of college kids, which is a lot of fun and has provided more interesting stories.

Scary Hairy College Guy

I once met a man
Who thought he was tough,
But when I saw his hair,
I knew it'd be rough.

His hair was long
And incredibly dense.
Why he wanted his penis waxed
Didn't make sense.

I started out small
To get him adjusted
To the pain that was to come
Before he combusted.

I told him about
Men who have passed out
To boost his confidence
And reassure his doubt.

He couldn't believe
How his body was shaking;
He thought the experience
Was like an awakening!

For the first time in his life,
He admitted, to me, that
He couldn't feel his balls—
How could that be?

It has to make sense
Since I wax the whole area,
But it has to be better
Than a case of malaria.

He survived the assault
I performed on his junk.
Men getting Brazilians—
Who would have thunk?

ME waxes such a variety of people that it's hard to describe what goes through her mind on any particular day. That's one of the reasons I became a legitimate entity in ME's head. Let me give you a more in-depth look at what is going on and what she is thinking during random situations. For example, she had an obese woman come in for a wax, and she couldn't find her bikini area. In her head, I was chanting the most persistent mantra I have ever sung to her, "You're digging to China to find her vagina. You're digging to China to find her vagina. You're digging to China to find her vagina." It really felt like she was digging to China to find her promised land.

A few weeks later, she waxed a hairy Jewish lady. ME told her the story about China and included the fact that she had written a poem about it. This client wasn't as big, but she was really hairy. ME told the client that she was digging to Israel to try to find her promised land. The client thought it was one of the funniest things she had ever heard. So here it is.

Digging to China

I hope you don't mind—
I'll try to be kind—
But waxing your vagina
Is like digging to China.

It's so hard to start
When your legs are apart

And all I can see
Is the vast periphery.

Bodies can be strange,
And I try to arrange
Your legs in a way
I'll finish the same day.

So please try to stretch,
And I'll work hard to fetch
Your hair-free vagina
From the country of China.

Another source of both pleasure and income that ME has worked diligently on is her writing career. As you now know, she has now successfully written three *Happy* books. Even though she hasn't made a ton of money on the books, she loves that she has made thousands of people laugh with her stories. You can't put a price on that. That doesn't mean she doesn't hope to one day. She'd be lying if she didn't admit that she hopes her books will become popular. Who wouldn't dream of monetary success when she's worked so hard doing something that makes her happy? She loves writing about her crazy profession. Ripping for a living has provided her with more joy than she could have imagined. It has been so rewarding for her to know that people enjoy reading what she writes. No matter how popular the *Happy* books get, she plans to continue writing.

ME loves the word happy. She loves being happy. She wishes more people could find happiness all year long. In fact, she just had the word *felice* tattooed on her low back. It means always happy in Italian. Yep, that sounds about right. One day, she reflected on how happiness can correlate to several of the holidays throughout the year. I guess it was her distorted way of associating something sexy and positive with each major holiday. It's a little random, but I kind of like it.

The Holiday Hoo-Ha

Nude for New Year's
Vajazzled for Valentine's Day
Edible for Easter
Mouthwatering for Mother's Day
Finger-licking good for Father's Day
Insatiable for Independence Day
Luscious for Labor Day
Horny for Halloween
Thermal for Thanksgiving
Cumming for Christmas
Truly a Happy Holiday Hoo-Ha

Another reason ripping for a living makes her happy is because it's a lot of fun. She laughs all day long. We both do. It's not hard to believe considering the utterly bizarre career choice she picked. It's a shame more people don't enjoy their jobs more. It would force people to lighten up and smile more and, ultimately, allow people to be happier.

When ME was a schoolteacher, she believes she did a commendable job. But she found it stressful, and it was impossible for her to not take the stress home. The pressures from teaching caused a lot of tension in her marriage. There were some ugly moments between Mr. and Mrs. Cleaver? Or should I say Mr. and Mrs. Beaver? (OK, that was a good one!) It's kind of good to know that this dynamic duo known as Mark and ME isn't quite as perfect as they seem.

There are definitely stressors in the salon business as well, but ME loves her job so passionately that she can deal with them a lot better. In other words, the stress that she deals with at work now is worth it.

When she thinks about all of the thousands of women she has waxed in her career, she wants to make up some kind of story to associate each person with. That's why she felt inclined to write the following poem.

Just Some Girls

Alice
Had a pussy like a palace;
Betty
Made me real hot and sweaty;
Chrissie
Handled it like a sissy;
Danielle
Did nothing but yell;
Eve
Thought I was going to break her beave;
Franny
Had the biggest white fanny;
Gayle
Couldn't wait to bail;
Harriet
Wanted sex with a prince on a chariot;
Isabel
Told me to go to hell;
Janice
Had a really big pannis;
Kelly
Had a really big belly;
Lynn
Took a few shots of gin;
Mary
Was freaking hairy;
Nancy
Thought her landing strip was fancy;
Olivia
Kicked me with her tibia;
Pearl
Had hair that could swirl;

Queenie
Said her man had a small weenie;
Ryan
Was almost crying;
Sally
Just wouldn't rally;
Terry
Had a vagina that was scary;
Ursula
Liked the word clitoral;
Victoria
Expected euphoria;
Wanda
Was the size of a Honda;
Xahia
Said her pussy smelled like a dahlia;
Yvette
Broke out into a sweat;
Zoe
Felt the pain from her head to her toey.

The final, and probably the most important, reason she enjoys ripping for a living is you. She has established incredible relationships with her clients over the years. It's really hard to put into words how important all of you have been in her life. The word meaningful only scratches the surface of what she feels for the clients who have shared a part of their lives with her. When you work in a service industry like ours, the relationships we establish with our clients are important. They make our job and our lives so much more meaningful. Our clients have become our friends and our families, and we care a lot about them. We believe you can never have too many people in your life who are important to you. It may sound a little schmaltzy, even though it comes from the heart. We can't thank the thousands of men and women who have come to our salon over the years. They have added so much to our lives.

Pussies, Pricks, and Pleasure

Pussies are soft and pretty and pink,
And they aren't quite as complicated as you may think.
Pricks can be soft, and they can be hard,
But women prefer when they're standing at guard.
Pleasure is really the ultimate prize,
But it can be hindered when the prick has no size.
Pussies, pricks, and pleasure, my friend,
Keep our species a-going until the bitter end.

It's impossible to not feel a connection with a woman when you have your hands between her legs and are hurting her (or him for that matter). It's a pretty intense bonding experience. So you probably can understand how special this whole thing is.

Clients share funny, sad, and even intimate things with us, and, believe it or not, there have been enough stories to write three full books about ME's experiences as a Brazilian-wax technician. Since this is the last book that she's writing about Brazilians, she wanted to share a few more of the stories to give you a better idea of what her days are like before she calls it quits on the crazy storytelling.

A client was gushing about the man she was in love with. She talked about many of the wonderful facets of their relationship, and it was hard to not be truly excited for her. She couldn't wait to tell ME when she knew he was the perfect man for her. We expected some kind of romantic tale that mimicked a modern-day love story. Wrong. She told us that she knew he was the man for her because his penis fit perfectly into her vagina. That response surprised ME more than you can imagine, which, by the way, is pretty hard to do. We started laughing, congratulated her, and wished her all the best.

The penis is an important part of a relationship. Women need it to work well. They need it to fit a certain way. They need it to be a certain size. Small can be completely ineffective or absolutely perfect. Too big can be really unpleasant or absolutely perfect as well. It's important for most women to check out the fine details of a penis before they commit to it. If a woman isn't totally into a penis, there's always the possibility that the relationship won't last. When women aren't satisfied in bed, they sometimes feel compelled to find the penis that is just right for them.

We've had a lot of men with uncircumcised penises come in to get Brazilians in the past two years. It has been a lot of fun to wax men, since the majority of our days are spent with women. We'd be lying if we didn't admit how surprised we've been by the number of uncircumcised men who come into the salon. Fortunately, we had an uncut man explain why it's so important for a man with an intact foreskin to remove all the hair on his penis. He told us that when there is hair on the shaft of the penis, it becomes tangled in the end of the penis as the erect penis becomes flaccid. He said it's uncomfortable when this happens. We can only imagine. He said that things are much nicer when the hair is removed. Now that Brazilians have become more popular for men, it has proven to be a great alternative to shaving.

A couple's anatomy needs to be compatible. Hell, the grooming ritual of each person's private parts can be a deal breaker. That is why so many people come to see us for a wax. We know that a lot of men and women have definite opinions about the pubic hair that they are going to sleep with. That's where we come in. We can help facilitate the process that makes the genitals more happy with one another.

We're not going to lie, but there are certain parts of the anatomy that can hurt like a motherfucker when you wax them. Believe it or not, there are other parts that don't hurt at all. Every body part feels things different and every person has a different tolerance to the ripping.

There was this chick who hung on to ME's hand like it was her lifeline while ME waxed her ass. It was pretty annoying and a part of ME (OK, a big part) that wanted to tie her down. Didn't she know that the puckered skin around the rectum is really tough and doesn't have many nerve endings? Most people say they love having the hair around their asshole waxed because it doesn't hurt at all.

Since the client was holding ME's hand, she wasn't holding up her left cheek, which was her job at that point of the appointment. This is the only time during a Brazilian that ME requires a client to help her out, unless the client is really, really big. Spreading your cheeks shouldn't be such a big deal. In this case, it was.

It was virtually impossible to get to that tiny hole that nestles in the dark caverns of this particular client. We've talked about it now in the first two books, on our helpful wax hint page on our website, and now again in this book. Stop fighting ME. Commit or don't commit. It's a black-or-white decision. There is no gray matter in the equation at all. OK, sometimes there's some discolored matter in the equation. Ugh. Make the decision one way or another. Do you want a smooth, cleaner, hair-free butt or not? If you want it done, then just lie there, lift your ass cheek, and let ME do her job. It only takes like forty seconds. She has no desire to spend a lot of time back there. It's not her favorite part of the body by any means. If you're really nervous, buy some numbing cream to desensitize the area a bit. Other than that, we don't know how to beg for your cooperation. You could buy handcuffs. It seems to be all the rage these days. So ME did the best that she could and moved on.

As you can tell, ME likes rhymes and singsong phrases. They make her smile and bring even more levity into our fun-filled days. When she asks a client to roll on their right side, many don't know their rights from their lefts. That's when she tells them to just give her their asses. There are a few different expressions she uses when waxing that area, and we thought you might get a kick out of them.

Give Me Your Ass

1.) Lift it like you mean it,
So it's easier to clean it.

2.) You better lift your heinie,
So I can make it nice and shiny.

3.) Spread it nice and wide,
'Cause there's nothing left to hide.

4.) Show me your anus;
It could make you famous.

5.) There is no decorum
When you show me your rectum.

6.) Spread it,
So I can thread it.

7.) Give me your ass,
So I can get rid of your grass.

It's funny, because somebody actually asked us if our Happy Hoo-Ha Numbing Cream made anal sex better. I don't know. I haven't tried it for that particular purpose (which probably surprises you since I tend to swing that way.) Feel free to let us know what you find out. Inquiring minds want to know.

As we mentioned earlier, ME has been writing a blog called *Hose Down Your Hoo-Ha* for several years. Maybe if we keep mentioning it, you may start following it. Hint. Hint. There aren't many people who wax men and women's genitalia for a living, so we feel obligated to share some of the more amusing stories with the public. Genitalia? How PC of us. (Politically correct, not personal computer, my friends.) Every day we share some kind of random story that happened to us at work with our followers. It's hard for us to hold things back and not share them.

Who could ever forget the first time a lady peed on ME? It was pretty surreal. She couldn't wait to blog about it the next day, because she had waxed thousands of women in her career and that had never happened before. How could we not share it? It's humbling for us to say that we have a lot of dedicated followers who say they look forward to reading her blog every day. Maybe they're just saying that since she is the person who puts hot wax between their legs. I think I'd say nice shit to my wax lady too, even if I didn't read her blog.

Even when ME traveled overseas, she made sure to continue with the blog on a daily basis. It is such a cool feeling to know you can make someone smile with one of your absurd stories. Her persistence in maintaining the blog for so many years has been commendable. She may sound like a compulsive nut job, but...

We probably shouldn't boast about her consecutive blogging on an almost daily basis since it only reinforces how bad her OCD is. She has missed only a handful of days, and it causes her anxiety. We aren't trying to say that OCD is necessarily a problem. OK, maybe a little problem. It's just who she is. Besides, they do say that people with obsessive-compulsive disorder tend to be productive and successful. No one will argue that ME isn't productive, but, if you are so productive, why aren't you a fucking millionaire?

Giving a client a thorough Brazilian is satisfying. It makes ME feel like she has successfully completed a marathon. Anything less than a Brazilian makes her feel incomplete and a bit unsatisfied and almost sad. Sometimes she likes to use analogies to describe her angst.

Running to Brazil

A 5K run
Reminds me
Of that first bikini wax:

It's short and sweet
And covers a small area,

But I always feel
Like I should have run a little farther.

A 10K run
Reminds me
Of that first *Playboy* wax:

It's a skinny landing strip
That reflects a longer sojourn.

You take a bigger risk—
Take a little more hair—
And wonder how much farther you can go.

A marathon
Reminds me
Of the ultimate adventure:

There's such satisfaction
When you run the whole way.
There's no greater high.

Running to Brazil
Will be
The best run of your life.

One day, ME had an MRI on her knee. Since she's highly claustrophobic, she needed her husband, Mark, in the room with her for moral support. Mark has been exposed to whatever creepy rays or magnetic thingies are emitted into the air nine times so far, and none of them involved him getting into the machine. Is that a good husband or what?

Anyways, the woman who came in the room to inject her with the contrast dye recognized ME right away. ME had given her a Brazilian a few years back. The woman had referred a friend to come see us. When the friend left the salon, she'd called the woman to tell her that her pussy looked like a red tomato.

Shortly thereafter, this friend went with her husband to buy a boat. Ironically, the boat happened to be red. When they got it home, they brainstormed what to name their new vessel, and they considered naming it the *Red Tomato*!

It fascinates me how a ten-minute service can permeate into so many different facets of people's lives. How cool would it be to name a boat after your first waxing experience? Radical.

Women have all kinds of different sayings and phrases when they come to see ME with regard to the service that they will be getting done. One girl told us that she always refers to an appointment at Mark & M. E. as "going to brunch." That is probably one of our favorite expressions to date, since getting a Brazilian wax often leads to a lot more oral sex. If you are one of those women who are in a committed relationship and don't receive cunnilingus on a regular basis, maybe you should consider taking a trip to Mount Hope Avenue in Rochester, New York. We may be able to help you out with that one. It's just a suggestion.

If you'd like another brilliant suggestion from the peanut gallery, we think you should encourage your mate to do what dozens of couples are doing at Mark & M. E. It has become popular for dating and married couples to come in for side-by-side Brazilians. This way, both partners can experience what it feels like to get waxed. We have found that sharing such an intense experience can be a type of foreplay. It is also interesting for people to experience getting a Brazilian with their partners in the room.

ME told one couple that sex would be so much better after they got a wax, because they would both be smooth and hairless. When they came back the second time, the guy told her that she couldn't have been any more accurate. He said sex was so much more sensual without the hair or the prickly feeling of shaved or trimmed hair between them. Told ya so!

Silky Sex

If you have sex
In a hair-free zone,
Prepare yourself
For a big, fat moan,
'Cause sex is better
When it is smooth
And it's so much easier
To find that groove.
Just cry and scream
And moan in lust,

'Cause a hair-free zone
Is a definite must.

When you rip hair out of people's bodies for a living, there are hazards you may encounter throughout the day. The repercussions from inflicting pain onto others can be visibly seen on ME's body. One woman grabbed her right forearm with both of her hands and twisted her skin. ME wasn't sure what the twisting motion was about, but it was pretty obnoxious, and it kind of hurt. A few hours later, there were large scratches on her arm that lasted for a couple weeks. Every job has its hazards, but who would think a woman would claw ME like a rabid animal? Considering what she does to people, it's not that farfetched a concept.

This story reminds me of something that happened when ME transferred to the University Of Rochester in 1984. She was sitting at a bar close to campus and heard about AIDS for the first time. It was like the threat of AIDS seemed so real overnight. Everybody became paranoid about coming in contact with someone else's blood. It was a scary time in our history. When she first became sexually active, the only things she worried about were herpes or unwanted pregnancies. She never thought that having sex could be life threatening. It was terrifying.

Even though AIDS still exists and is still a threat, I can't say that we've ever really worried that we could be legitimately exposed to it during a wax session. Then the lady who kneaded ME's forearm like dough came in for an appointment. That's when this whole AIDS thought became a valid worry. It made her uncomfortable to know that this lady scratched her skin hard enough to make her bleed, and then subsequently scab. She wondered if she should consider an AIDS test.

That wasn't the first time clients made her bleed. Several women over the years have clawed at her with their natural and artificial nails. Who would have thought that waxing v-jays for a living could be so risky?

There are many times when we tell people about something that happened in the wax room, and we wish they could have seen it for themselves. We started thinking that illustrations of some of the crazy shit that happens during a wax would make the stories more fun. A friend of ours introduced us to this talented man named Brian Robbins who offered to help us illustrate some of the funnier scenarios. When he first agreed to draw pictures for us in *The Happy Hen House*, I don't think he realized how invaluable his talent was to us. When we thought about writing *The Happy Trail*, we couldn't wait to have him draw some new pictures. Our subject matter may be a little off-color, but he accepted his drawing assignments in the second book like a champ, and made them even funnier in the process.

In *The Happy Hen House*, we told a story about our desire to write a coffee-table book about hemorrhoids called *Rectal Cornucopia*. You see, we see a lot of hemorrhoids every day and want men and women to be less self-conscious about them. They don't gross us out. We just work around them. It's no big deal. We asked Brian to draw an illustration of a cornucopia growing out of a woman's buttocks. Not only did he draw a large cornucopia protruding out of the woman's butt, he had ME riding it! When we saw the illustration the first time, we were screaming because it was so funnier then we could have ever imagined. We are definitely a good team, and we hope you enjoy the illustrations that he did for us in this book as well.

One day, this girl came in all wired up about getting her first Brazilian. She was young and slender, and ME didn't think that waxing her would be a problem. That was the first mistake. Trust me; you have to watch out for the skinny ones. They sometimes fight like wild animals. She was one of them.

When ME asked her to lift up her leg, she was worried about getting kicked in the head. The girl's reaction was even worse than that. She slammed the leg that was in the air onto ME's back and pulled her down into a scissor hold. It was an extremely awkward wrestling move that ME could not get out of. ME was seriously pinned between the girl's legs, and her face was much closer to her lady parts than she was comfortable with. So I'd like to introduce you to her first encounter with being put in a scissor hold.

The next time this girl came in (yep, she came back), she walked in the room and reminded ME that she was the scissor-hold girl. Believe me when I say that she was hard to forget. There is something memorable about a

Robbins 2015

woman who forces your face in her crotch. Fortunately, we're happy to report that we didn't wrestle the second time.

The first time is always the hardest. Kind of like losing your virginity.

Some people find it impossible to not be theatrical while they're getting a wax. There is so much God talk in the wax rooms that we don't need to wear our crucifix anymore. The references to Jesus, Jesus Christ, and God are constant. There is often incessant praising and praying and just a lot of random God-related chatter. It often consumes the entire service.

The church service often begins before we even start putting the wax on the skin, and it continues until we lay the clients on their sides. We support any ranting that comes out of a man or woman's mouth if that is what it takes for the client to muster the courage to make it through the appointment. Even if you aren't a religious person, you'd be amused at what goes on at the church of ME.

The only time we wished we had our crucifix on was when we needed God's assistance. For example, when someone has a leg on ME's back, and it feels heavy, we pray for the strength to finish that side of the body so we can have the client put the leg down. OK, we should probably just admit that there are times we want chicks to stop pushing their tree trunks of legs and get off our backs or tell the skinny ones to stop trying to scissor hold us. Been there. Done that. But, for the most part, we don't rely on God to get us through our day. We focus on laughter and experience to help us muster through.

We would be remiss if we didn't admit that there are times when we'd like to use our crucifix to perform an exorcism on the dingleberries and other assorted foreign objects that join us during the waxing service. ME's crucifix came from Italy, so it must have a fair amount of power. But we need to shelve this discussion, because we promised no more nasty stories. We're ending on a funny note. Remember?

ME's ripping for a living can be helpful to people who have had surgery or have some kind of deformity. When a woman has had her breasts removed because of breast cancer, it changes the shapes of her underarms and makes it difficult for her to shave that area. A plastic surgeon referred a woman to ME to wax her underarms for that exact reason. Since then, she has also started waxing her bikini line. The first time she waxed that area, she was not a happy camper. She told ME that at least when she had surgery, they gave her good drugs. She also commented that IV sedation might not be a bad idea either. Women can be such drama queens sometimes.

Since ME is able to wax all her body parts herself, she doesn't have to shave anything. She can't stand razor burn or stubble, and now that her skin is older, it tends to get really irritated by a razor. One day, she had this adorable red-haired woman tell her that she started shaving again to save money. It is definitely a monetary commitment to get waxed on a regular basis. She couldn't deal with all the irritation she got from the razor. In fact, she said that starting to shave again was one of the worst decisions of her life. That seems a little over the top, but we'll go with it. So her New Year's resolution was to never shave again. Yep, that's our kind of girl. Before she left the salon, she told ME that she couldn't believe she preferred to wax herself. She wanted to know if she had a suicide wish.

It is incredible how some of the most flexible women lose all sense of flexibility in the wax room. ME was waxing this yoga instructor who had pretty much psyched herself out before they even started. There was a fair amount of swearing aimed at our dutiful technician and at the client's friend, who was sitting in the hallway. When she was instructed to perform a one-legged "Happy Baby" which is a common yoga move, she had the hardest time opening up her hips and getting into the position. We gave her a hard time about not being able to do this move when she yelled, "I fucking hate the Happy Baby!" And there you have it. One of the most un-Zen-like responses to such an adorably named yoga position could not be achieved by even the most qualified yogis.

Women like to be prepared for their first Brazilian, and many don't know what being prepared really entails. If you read some of the stuff we write, you know your hair has to be long enough, you should be clean, you should be hydrated, and the list goes on. Many women have a preconceived notion about will happen before, during, and even after a wax. A repeat client brought in a friend to get a wax. While they waited for the appointment, the regular client noticed that her friend had an extra pair of panties in her purse. She asked her why she brought another pair of underwear with her. The friend said she wanted to be prepared. Since she was so nervous about the wax, she was afraid she would pee herself. Wouldn't be the first time, and most certainly won't be the last.

Speaking of men's and women's anatomy...we had a man come in for a Brazilian who wanted to know why God had put the picnic next to the sewage dump. That's a valid question. He said it was disturbing mostly because his wife wouldn't sit and eat at his picnic. The whole discussion of pussies, pricks, and pleasure can be complicated you know.

ME the Comedienne

It's hard to keep up with what ME is doing at any one time. She has an itchy personality and always has to be doing something. And she has done some pretty random shit in her time. She's been an aerobics instructor, nail technician, elementary-school teacher, wax technician, author, and, most recently, a stand-up comedienne. What's next? Who the hell knows? She's always planning something new and different to do. Her biggest problem is trying to narrow down where she wants to direct her efforts. There are so many options and not enough time to do everything she wants to do. And, oh yeah, you did read it right. ME did stand-up at our local comedy club in Rochester, New York. In fact, you can watch her performance on YouTube. It's called *The Happy Hoo-Ha Live*!

Her goal was to tell stories from all three of her books and hope it would fill about twenty minutes of time and be funny, of course. Well, if you have ever met ME, she is a talker. And she doesn't shut up sometimes. Instead of telling stories for twenty minutes, she rambled on for a whopping twenty-nine minutes! And the kicker is that she didn't even tell half the jokes she had written down.

She had taken her two oldest children to see David Koechner at the Comedy Club the week before, and, since he had jokes written down, she figured it wouldn't be tacky to do the same thing. But as she was talking, she kept remembering incidents in her life that were even funnier than those she had written down, so she went with them.

The show was called *The Rage Against the Vageen*. It's a monthly event at our local comedy club put together by a local comedienne, Madelein Smith, to showcase local female comediennes. ME was fortunate enough to be the headliner on the November 19, 2014. Madelein had been putting this show on for over a year, and she was gracious enough to let ME get up on stage and tell some stories.

Madelein was worried that ME wouldn't have enough material to fill twenty minutes of time. She obviously didn't have a clue who she was talking to. ME could have easily talked for an hour. Madelein offered a question-and-answer point in the routine if ME couldn't fill enough time, but that was so not necessary. Getting ME to shut up would be Madelein's biggest feat.

Since there were mostly women in the audience, it was hard not to notice the few men who attended. When the show started, Madelein singled out ME's son Adryan and asked him what brought him to the event. He proudly said that he was the son of the Brazilian Wax Queen. ME was overjoyed by her son's praise and description. In fact, it was hard for her to not get a little choked up by it. As it turned out, the comics harassed Adryan throughout the evening, which he took in stride and with great humor.

When ME was on stage, she remembered a funny story about Adryan and thought it would be fun to share it since everyone knew who he was. The first time she gave Adryan a Brazilian (yes, they are a close family), he called her a whore. Let me explain. When she lifted his leg up to wax underneath his scrotum, he sat up and, in the most demonic voice, called her a whore. She proceeded to lie him back down and let him know that he shouldn't call his mommy a whore.

What ME didn't realize was that Mark didn't know that their eldest son had called her a whore, and she heard him laughing hysterically in the audience. It was definitely one of the highlights of the evening.

The next day, ME saw her daughter Kaylah at the gym. Kaylah had also been in the room when Adryan got waxed that first time. (Close-knit family, remember?) She had forgotten that he called ME a whore. (How could she forget?) But she said that ME sounded as possessed as Adryan did the day it happened. She also remarked on how much Mark laughed through the performance. That made ME feel incredible. It takes a lot to get Mark to laugh sometimes.

A lot of Mark & M. E. clients assumed that stand-up comedy was something that ME had always wanted to do. But that wasn't the case at all. In fact, prior to meeting Madelein, ME had never put much thought into the telling-jokes-in-public thing. But when the opportunity presented itself, it seemed like a pretty cool gig to add to the bucket list that didn't evolve until ME was in her early forties. The first thing on her bucket list was to write a book. That evolved into the desire to write three books. Then the stand-up thing got thrown in just for fun. She has a few things lingering in the back of her brain that may or may not get added to the list, but none of them are so pressing that she feels the need to commit to them yet.

Whether or not ME is a valid comedienne is still up for debate. But you have to give the girl credit for trying. She ended her night with a poem about an unfortunate incident she had with a man named Bill. I know you'll feel for this guy. This was a hard day for poor old Bill.

Bill's Bleeding Balls

Bill was a man who had hair on each ball.
He wasn't too short and he wasn't too tall.
He had a great sense of humor and didn't mind the pain,
Even though his balls were bleeding like torrents of rain.

The first time he waxed was no big deal,
But something happened the second time that broke the seal.
The wax made him bleed like a fountain of red,
And all ME could do was feel tons of dread.

Bill saw her angst and tried to calm her down,
But the blood was excessive, and it made her frown.
If she could have held pressure that would have been handy,
It was like trying to press down on pink cotton candy!

It is hard to wax an area when it's all wet,
And it didn't help that the blood made ME sweat,

But Bill was a champ of the very best kind.
He wanted her to finish; he had the results in mind.

Later that day he called the shop
To say everything was OK; the blood had stopped.
ME was relieved and exhaled a big sigh…
Sometimes it's stressful to wax a guy.

Fearless of the Fur

A lady told ME that it felt like she shoved a Popsicle stick up her ass while she was waxing those pesky little hairs around her rectum. Well, if we're being honest—which we usually are to a fault—we get pretty damn close to going up your ass. Hair grows out of the anal region like a budding flower, and no matter how much you like flowers, they shouldn't have hair on them. So we go for it, because we're fearless of the ass.

I didn't think we'd dedicate any more time to stories regarding the ass, like in *The Happy Hen House*, but there were enough things that happened that made it necessary to write at least a short chapter on the subject. Besides, this whole butt thing is pretty comical if you think about it.

One girl came in and said that ME put her in "ouchy pose" when she lifted her leg up. The whole *ouchy* word sounded like a pretty juvenile expression, but women often act out of the ordinary when they are assuming the position with no panties on. Besides, lifting a leg up can be uncomfortable for a lot of our clients, because so many people have tight hamstrings. But that's not the funny part of the story...We'd like to hope that making a woman uncomfortable isn't the funny part, anyway.

When ME rolled the client on her side, the woman said she felt like she was in a *Hustler* pose. Even after all of ME's years of rolling women on their sides, no one has ever referred to that position as "a Hustler." We don't find the position pornographic or sexy, but sure, we final all analogies interesting. If the woman felt like a porn star, all the power to her. I'd be lying if I didn't comment that my first thought was that this woman probably wasn't too creative in bed if she felt like a porn star while rolling on her side and lifting up her left butt cheek, but who am I to judge?

In most cases, women have bigger butts then men. The wider hips are so much more conducive to bearing children, but they can make things more complicated in the wax room. And there are some women who have ridiculously large butts. You know, the kind of butts that have had songs written about them. A woman told us that she couldn't hold up her cheek because it was so sweaty. We do make people sweat, but that wasn't the only reason she couldn't hold up her cheek. It was freaking huge. Yep, her butt was most definitely worthy of a song. So we tried to hold it up, but it just wasn't happening. In times like this, we often wonder if we are getting weaker or if the parts keep getting bigger. The point of this commentary is to point out that if you cannot hold your own cheek up, don't expect us to wax that area. We can't wax what we can't see. I think that's a law of physics or some kind of science.

One day, a young college girl told us that she always feels like Beyoncé when she gets a Brazilian. Since this girl had a pretty big caboose, the first thing we thought of was whether it was possible that when we removed her pubic hair, her butt would look even larger. We tried to conceptualize the correlation between the two even if it didn't make any sense. As it turns out, that isn't what she meant at all. ME asked her why she feels like Beyoncé every time she gets waxed. She said that Brazilians make her feel sexy and, in her opinion, no one is sexier than Beyoncé. No arguments here.

It's funny, because that story reminds us of something another young woman said. She said that when you see a hot guy, you aren't supposed to refer to the excited feeling you get as getting butterflies in your stomach. She said that the new expression is called "pussy-flies." Of course, we thought the expression was brilliant. Any creative way to use the word pussy is always a plus in our book. Gee, I wonder if the other girl we were just talking about gets "pussy-flies" over Beyoncé? Interesting question.

Pussy-flies

Pussy-flies are perfect
In every single way.
They are the indication
You want to fuck all day.
So when you get those flutters
Right between your legs,
Don't be surprised
If your pussy begs.
For a big fat cock
And a nice solid thrust
That can take you to heaven
From your pussy to your bust.

We're pretty fearless of the fur no matter what time of the month it is. In fact, we are always amused by the women who refer to their period week as "shark week." We've told funny stories about this before, because we think it's a pretty amusing description of that time of the month. That expression reminded us of something that happened one day. ME was watching the movie *Jaws* on her big-screen television in a family room that she ironically calls the "shark room" since it was built in 1995. In case you're wondering why it is called that, let me explain. It's kind of a cool story.

In 1989 Mark went deep-sea fishing with ME's dad and two friends, and they caught a huge Mako shark. It was an exciting day. That night, they had quite a drunken celebration with way too many pitchers of rum runners. After they brought the shark on shore, Mark hired a taxidermist in the Florida Keys, which is where he caught the shark, to make a replica of it to put in their house. It's hard to find a spot in the house for an eight-foot shark, so they built a room for it. Since they don't have much of a basement and needed place for the kids to hang out, this room became vital to the development of their dream house. It's actually the most awesome room. They have a bar, pool table, poker table, wraparound couches, slot and pinball machines...

you get the drift. Basically, it's the room where all the vagabond teenagers hung out when they were growing up.

Sadly, ME lost her dad in a tragic accident two days after the big catch, so the shark room kind of memorialized his memory as well as provided them with a kick-ass family room. Surround sound is connected to the television in the room. It's a cool feature that adds to the suspense of scary or violent movies. This is particularly exciting and kind of scary when you watch *Jaws* for the first time.

While ME was watching the scene where the camera is only zoomed on the lower half of the people's bodies and the famous music played in the background, all she could think of was that men are like sharks. When a woman gets a Brazilian, they become obsessed with the lower part of her body and if you use your imagination, you can almost hear the music as they get ready to sink their teeth into you. Isn't that what you thought of the last time you saw *Jaws*?

Since we've alluded to that special time of the month, which can get messy, we might as well continue with a nasty story for those of you sickos who crave the dirt like we all secretly do. An M. E. Nesser book would not be complete without a gross "between the cheeks" story. When gross shit happens, she tends to blog about it. That isn't entirely accurate. People like the gross stories, so she *does* blog about everything unpleasant that happens in the wax room. After she had an "incident" with an unpleasant backside, this is what she blogged. Bowel movement, bath, Brazilian. In that order. We thought it was a straightforward, to the point, and fairly poignant explanation of the order with which these tasks need to be dealt with.

One day, we had a couple in the room for side-by-side Brazilians. As we mentioned earlier, it's becoming a popular service at Mark & M. E. Creative foreplay we like to think...When the man rolled onto his side, it was an absolute mess. It was disgusting. It was inexcusable, discourteous, and pretty fucked up. We wanted to throw up. How could he go to an appointment that deals with removing all of the hair between his cheeks without washing the area first? We just don't get it. It made us completely enraged. We felt compelled to remain professional and keep the light, upbeat conversation going so he didn't feel embarrassed when all we wanted to do was smack him upside the head!

I guess one of the suggestions that we'd like to make is to tell your man get rid of the hair between his cheeks so that nothing ever gets left behind. You could also teach him to use disposable wipes, or suggest that he take a shower after a bowel movement. Or how about this idea? Tell him to feel free to shove the garden hose up his ass after he takes a shit! Blood-pressure check please.

Everyone has a different reaction to pain. Some people's bodies start to shake from the adrenalin surge, and they cannot control it. We try to reassure the clients who shake that it is totally normal, but many get embarrassed. We tried to convince one client that it wasn't fear. It was her body getting excited about her wax. She didn't buy that theory, but we had a good laugh over it.

There is one Mark & M.E. client who hangs onto ME's ass while she gives them a Brazilian. Since she has her hands between their legs, it's only fair that the woman hangs onto her ass. Some women apologize when they grab her, but keep their hands there anyways. Others couldn't care less. They just need something to hold. One woman told us that she had a death grip on her prey. I guess ME was the wild animal (or the prey) that was terrorizing her twat.

Getting waxed while you are pregnant is becoming more routine at the salon. There are definite considerations when we are working on an expectant mommy. Things change between the legs, so we have to be a lot more careful with what we're doing. A woman who was in her twenty-seventh week walked into the room, put her hands on her hips, and told me that she desperately needed our help. She had something growing out of her ass, and it was freaking her out. She said she couldn't see it and wanted us to look at it and tell her what is was. She had felt it and did an online search of hemorrhoids, and she didn't think that's what was growing there.

As soon as she got on the table, she wanted our opinion. We gave her the Brazilian, and when she turned on her side, we told her that it was a fissure. She yelled, "What the fuck is a fissure?" So while she cleaned up, we looked up fissures on our phone and read her the description. We love it when we actually do know the answer to something.

As you can see, you need to be fearless. You never know what you'll find when you're going down under.

Babble from the Bush

Since this is the last book about ME's experiences as a Brazilian-wax technician, we've decided to be as frank and as honest as possible so that readers can truly understand how bizarre and utterly outlandish this job really is. We find it amusing how people regularly pat themselves on the back for having the stamina to endure this taxing salon service. Many women like to compare each appointment with how they did at their last appointment. The funny thing is that, in our opinion, most of these women have a distorted view about how they behaved during the service.

One day, ME waxed a young woman who was extremely proud of how she handled her Brazilian. She reminded ME that it was her second time getting a wax. This time around, she applauded herself for only yelling for Jesus during her service. You see, the first time she came in, she cried for all of the twelve apostles. Sounds like progress to me. Although many women scream for Jesus during their waxes, the whole apostle thing was a new one. It was really funny.

Animated is a great description of how a lot of women behave during a wax. If a woman isn't holding her breath or swearing like a truck driver, chances are she's acting in some animated fashion. On the one hand, a little animation can be amusing. On the other hand, it's fucking annoying. So let's give all the theatrical ladies a piece of advice. Spit out the extra cups of coffee. Caffeine is dehydrating and makes your pores more resistant to extraction. More importantly, it makes you more nervous and jittery. This artificial stimulation often accentuates your nervous behavior and will make you more likely to act in a spastic fashion. For the record, spastic is obnoxious. Coffee seems to be most women's liquid of choice, but it is not recommended prior to a wax. If it's nerves that make you anxious, try meditation, calming mental imagery or even such chamomile tea before you come in.

Not only does caffeine dehydrate your skin, so does perspiration. Since we tend to make you sweat, being dehydrated is really not a smart idea. We don't mind when a person sweats during the service as long as the skin doesn't get so wet that the wax won't stick to it. The wax will absolutely not stick to a wet surface. We've learned this not-so-minor fact about the science of waxing a long time ago, and, no matter how sophisticated wax is made, it still won't adhere to a wet surface.

One woman became totally embarrassed because there was a pool of sweat in her belly button. Unfortunately, some clients are sweating before they even undress. We honestly couldn't believe how fast her belly button filled up. It was pretty amusing. At one point, we had to get a towel and dry her off so we could get the wax to stick to her skin. It was kind of a pain, in case you were wondering.

Wet can present itself in the form of other substances besides sweat when men and women enter the red room of pain. One of our waxing suites is red, and 'Red Room of Pain' is one of the names it has been called in the past. A girl was sniffling, and her nose was running, so we handed her a Kleenex tissue. We decided we'd rather deal with a runny nose than a runny...

Gooey

Ooey, gooey,
Forget about being chewy—
Any extra mess
Makes me want to mutilate your nest.
Clean your shit
Before you come in,
So I can wax you proper
Without a fake grin.

Women today are expected to be stronger and more capable. That's probably why a client told us that if she were a Victorian lady, she would have fainted. For the record, we do not like fainters at Mark & M. E. In this instance, we are celebrating that she wasn't a Victorian lady.

Women are funny when they haven't been waxed in a while and like to compare their pubic hair to something random before we even see it. A woman referred to her bush as a rabid animal. Did we think it resembled one? Well, maybe. It was pretty scary. After she said that, we were a little afraid that some kind of animal would jump out of it. No worries, ME, genital crabs are on the verge of extinction. I think you're safe. She must have found the abundance of hair objectionable in order to call it rabid. We just knew it'd take a little more energy to rip out. That's why we take our vitamins.

It is incredible how unique every client is and how unique everyone's pubic hair is. I find the hair and the roots that attach themselves onto the wax strip absolutely fascinating. Sometimes the roots are huge. Sometimes they're barely visible. Some strips may be covered in a ton of thick, black hair. Other strips have thin and fine hair dispersed on it.

One client wanted to see her strip. She was fascinated by it too, but she was also pretty grossed out by it. She said it reminded her of sticky flypaper. It's disgusting to see the dead flies on the paper, but it's also intriguing, and you can't help but look at it. It's like a crime scene. You know you shouldn't look, but you can't help yourself.

Speaking of animals, we got a little nervous when a woman came in and said she brought us her wolf pack. It was an interesting analogy. Our first thought was that "wolf pack" was what the group of guys called themselves in the movie *The Hangover*. ME's stream of consciousness continued with the thought that she'd love Bradley Cooper between her legs. Sometimes it's amusing to piggyback an innocent reference to a more provocative idea. The funny part of the story is that when the client took her pants off, ME told her she *could* probably hide a pack of wolves in her mound. It was ferocious.

Ferocious was how this woman sounded after she babbled in some exotic tongue, and then cackled like a hyena during her service. If you could only be a fly on the wall during some of these appointments, you'd know these stories are gospel. All of this animal talk is leading up to another poem.

The Howling Hoo-Ha

What is that creature
Sitting on your lap?
Is it some kind of animal
Taking a nap?

Or is it really
Just your pubic hair,
Who didn't get the memo
About going bare?

I'm a little afraid
About what I may see
When I search for your hoo-ha
Begging to be free.

I think you may be
Going undercover,
Because you could disguise
Yourself as another.

I hate to tell you,
But this is gonna hurt—
When I dig up the bush
I pray there's no dirt.

You may be tender
For a day or two;
Bald is a sensation
That'll be new to you.

So let's kill that beast
With a grunt and a growl,
Before your hoo-ha
Starts to howl.

You know you're getting older when your pubic hair turns gray. This is another good reason why you should remove all of the hair between your legs so that no one ever knows. You can color your pubic hair, but that is complicated and messy. It's easier to wax it all. Every once in a while, someone verbalizes a brilliant statement about gray pubes that needs to be shared. A woman told us that a silver beaver is not as distinguished as a silver fox. Amen, sister! It's not a fair statement, but it's definitely accurate. Who has ever heard of a sophisticated snatch?

Everyone's tolerance for pain is different. We don't think Brazilians hurt, but there are many girls who end up writhing in pain and crying. We would never criticize someone for what they feel. If they think it really kills, then it does. We may use humor as a distraction, but we believe the pain is real for many people.

One girl found her wax really unpleasant, but then she said that it was all good, because we were preparing her for her next tattoo. We love when we can be beneficial in more ways than one.

A boyfriend wanted to know what his girl's face looked like when she got a wax. As we started to wax her, she snapped two pictures of her face as she writhed in pain. Then she threw the phone across the room and said, "That's enough." She wasn't giving him any more than that. She said that was how she dealt with her anger-management issues.

We wrote several stories about Groupon nightmares in our last book and didn't want to talk about them again, but we have to tell you about a girl we met. One more story won't hurt, and this is a pretty crazy one. A girl came to us for a Brazilian. It took about ten minutes, and she was good to go. Then she got a twenty-five-dollar Groupon at another salon for a half leg and Brazilian and decided it was a great deal that she had to try. After two hours of hell, she couldn't leave that salon fast enough. A service like that would have taken about twenty minutes at our salon.

She said she had a three-hour drive after she left that salon, which was a nightmare because she was in so much pain that it hurt to physically sit in the car. We can't even imagine what they did to her, but she swore she would never go back. We have to admit that a part of us likes it when people go elsewhere, because it usually makes us feel even better about the way we do it. But in this case, we'd like to bitch-slap the girl who took so long to wax my client and left her parts so jacked up. There's no excuse for a half leg and Brazilian to take over two hours. It is unacceptable and inexcusable. She most definitely should have been able to sit down after it was over.

It takes a fair amount of inner strength and fortitude to endure someone putting hot wax between your legs. We had a woman confess that, as an overweight woman, Brazilians made her feel empowered. She didn't feel as heavy after a wax. She knew it was silly, but getting a wax made her feel skinnier. She walked more confidently after a wax and people even asked her if she lost weight. Maybe she walked more confidently without that big furry animal between her legs.

We agree that Brazilians are empowering and marvel on a daily basis the positive impact they have on people's lives. It's about way more than kick-ass sex, although the sexual benefits are amazing.

There can be negative aspects of getting a Brazilian, aside from the fact that they can be uncomfortable. *Uncomfortable?* For many, that is the most obscene understatement of the year. A client told us that the only negative side effect from getting a Brazilian is the change in urine stream. Her pee comes out differently? Interesting. We thought this declaration was pretty funny.

It was similar to the woman who told us that she had to be careful she didn't give herself a facial the first time she peed after a wax. Do you think they need to read the directions on the clean-up station a little more closely? She said it was something she dealt with every time she left the salon. We don't actually wax the urethra, so we're not sure how the changing urine stream works. We do know that she was not the first person to tell us it happens to her.

Most people wait longer between waxes in the winter. Face it; upstate New York is fucking cold. Most people aren't roaming around in bathing suits and booty shorts. It's hard to get motivated to go to a salon and get undressed when its single digits outside. This past winter, a woman came in and apologized for waiting so long. She begged us to remove her winter coat. We gladly obliged.

Someone came into the room looking like she wanted to ask a question, so we asked her what was up. She wanted to know why Mark was cutting hair. We've been asked a lot of strange questions in our career, but we thought this one was really peculiar. We told her that he has been a hairdresser for thirty-five years. She was totally shocked by this. She was under the impression that he was solely in charge of running the salon and making sure it ran well.

We have to admit he is good at that, but he has more than put his time in over the years. It never occurred to her that he did hair, because she usually came to the salon when he wasn't working or when he was running errands. We assured her that he was an excellent hairdresser and that if it weren't for him, ME would have never gotten into the business.

Then the woman commented on ME's hair. She said she always liked how she had it cut and wondered who cut it. We told her Mark had been cutting her hair for thirty years. She couldn't believe it. Duh...His name is on the sign, you know?

Want another brilliant comment that someone told us? One of our clients came in to get waxed when she was nine months pregnant. She told a friend that she was on her way to Mark & M. E. to get a wax, and the friend did not understand why she would get a wax while she was pregnant. She told her it seemed unnecessary since no one would see it.

ME has been pregnant three times, and she knows for a fact that you feel fat and sweaty when you're about to deliver a baby, and being hairy between your legs makes you feel even more gross. Furthermore, if you need a cesarean section, the nurse will have to shave you, and then, not only will you be sore from the surgery, but the hair will itch like a son of a bitch when it grows back. Those explanations have nothing to do with the brilliance of her statement, however. She said that she couldn't understand why anyone would get a wax before having a baby because no one would see it. Is she for real? The whole fucking world sees your crotch when you have a baby! And if you are lucky enough to have a baby at a teaching hospital like ME did, you might as well put a sign on it that reads "Free peep show!" (Or maybe it should say "Free puss show"?)

In our opinion, all women should get a wax in their ninth month. We understand a woman's trepidation to get it all waxed when she is that far along in her pregnancy because of the extra sensitivity factor, but if a woman needs to be stitched up for either a cesarean or an episiotomy, she will be thankful she had the foresight to remove her hair.

It was funny because a few days later, a woman came in who had just had a baby a couple weeks before. She said that she waxed at Mark & M. E. every month until about the seventh month, and then quit. She said that she totally regretted not getting waxed right before the birth. It appears that she tore badly, and they had to shave her down below before they stitched her up. She said she was absolutely miserable. She was bleeding for a few weeks, and the area was sore and itchy, but she had to be careful because she had stitches.

ME was one of those women who had to be shaved in order to get stitches. The whole shaving thing when having a baby was something she learned the hard way. It sucked, and she'd never want a repeat performance on how badly it felt after.

Baby Babble

When you're expecting,
You're going to get fat.
It's just how it works;
It's a matter of fact.
Your puss will swell.
Your puss will sweat.
No matter what you do,
Change is all you'll get.
So you've got more weight,
And you've got more heat.
Your boobs are huge;

You can't see your feet.
Your puss is always wet.
It'll feel pretty strange.
Embrace the engorgement;
It's part of the change.
This is more than you bargained for.
More than you thought.
Get over the fact
Things will never be as taut.
One thing you can do
To make it feel clean,
Is let ME in
To your folds and in between.
She'll get rid of the hair
That is giving such bother.
And make you feel better
About being a mother.

Going completely bald isn't always the look pregnant women want, so we're more than happy to leave some hair behind. We'll never stop being amazed at what women ask for. Believe it or not, we are still whipping up shapes for people, pregnant and not-pregnant. We don't know when it became popular to make a heart with your hands, but that's the signal we often get from people who want us to leave a cute little heart shape on them. It seemed to be the rage around Valentine's Day this year. It is requested off season as well.

We recently had a girl ask for a postage stamp. Once again, that was a new description. Basically, a postage stamp is the shape of a square. A small square is what we call a little Hitler. Fortunately, we knew what the shape of a postage stamp was. All we could think of was that she wanted someone to lick her stamp and deliver her something good. Yeah baby, that's a good one.

Science and the Snatch

Don't worry about us going into any kind of scientific drudgery in this chapter. We just want to share some observations that may sound a little like science or at least science-related. ME barely made it through biology before she quit taking science altogether. If they didn't talk about sex in biology, she would have probably failed the course.

We believe in that whole fight-or-flight response. It seems to be a natural, instinctive way of dealing with unpleasant situations. During a Brazilian wax encounter, when a client feels threatened by my dreaded Popsicle sticks, we are sure many of them would love to flee the room. That usually isn't an option since the clients are naked from the waist down when they have this epiphany. We agree that it would be great reality television to have women running and screaming from the wax rooms with no pants on, but that hasn't ever happened. A Hollywood entertainment company actually approached us about doing a reality show, but they were more interested in the drama in our hair salon. Sadly, we were too happy and drama-free. The juicy drama and naughty conversations happen in the wax room, but they weren't interested in doing a show that revolved around waxing. We were disappointed. It could have been a lot of fun, and it would have been great for book sales.

If a client isn't able to flee the room, then the next obvious choice is to fight the person who is hurting them. We've actually been tempted to take pictures of ME's arms, hands and thighs to show people the battle wounds she has endured. As she has gotten older, she bruises fairly easy, and a clutch hold on her forearm or her hip will do just that—bruise her. She also gets scratched fairly easy as well. She's had scratches last over a week due to the plethora of women who have tried to claw their way to China through the passageway of her right arm.

It's all good though. We aren't complaining. It's all a part of the experience. The client can't help needing something to hang onto, and ME's the most likely candidate. Not for nothing, ME, I think they subconsciously want to hurt you. Yeah, probably.

There's definitely a science to waxing, but is there a science behind the preparation to getting a wax? According to one of our clients, there is. She has a well-defined ritual that she goes through before every wax, and she honestly believes that the wax will not be as successful if she doesn't prepare properly. Before every Brazilian that she has gotten at Mark & M. E., she eats a Snickers candy bar, drinks a jug of water, and says a prayer.

She brought her mother in for a wax once, and we saw that she was scheduled to come in the next day. We told her we would fit her in so that she didn't have to come back to the salon. She said that was not an option because she hadn't performed her pre-wax ritual. We had to respect her for that.

Whatever it takes to get a client through an appointment is never judged. We would never mock anyone. (not for that, at least) I think we have all been put in situations where we needed to do certain things before we endured a given task. A lot of people have rituals that help them cope. If it's a Snickers bar helps her endure ten minutes with ME, then a Snickers bar it is. Claiming her ritual is science may be a little sketchy, but, in her mind, it is a necessary component to getting a Brazilian.

Even if a Snickers bar isn't exactly science, there are some fundamental logistics that are necessary when you decide to wax on a regular basis. For starters, you need to be able to pay for it. Some may think it is a luxury (although the feeling isn't luxurious), but we have always contended that it is, in many cases, a medical necessity. That being said, in our economy, there may be times when you can't afford to get it done for a while. We can totally empathize.

We do, however, like when people give us a heads-up when they decide to take a break. One client, who had been coming to us for years, sent us an e-mail to tell us that she had to give up a smooth landing in order to pay for her son's swimming lessons. We appreciated the message, but we secretly worried that she would be forced to put on a bathing suit with her dark pubic hair sticking out all over the place. After a two-month absence, she was able to get back on the plane and enjoy her smooth landing.

Everyone needs to stop worrying about getting injured when they get a Brazilian. Injuries are few and far between. If you get waxed by someone with experience, your risk is even lower. We had a woman worry that we had given her skin lacerations from the wax. We're not even sure how that's possible. Her skin was a little red. That was it. No scrapes, cuts, or wounds. No hemorrhaging. Ergo, no skin lacerations. We think it would help if more people focused on the end results and stopped lamenting about the actual ten-minute procedure. It would also probably help to focus on how soft and clean your skin will feel, how much better your panties will look without hair hanging out of the sides, and how much more intense your lovemaking is going to be. If that doesn't get you excited, I don't know what will.

Women are complicated creatures. Unlike men, they have inside and outside parts that can be fairly difficult to access. For the record, we try to be careful not to intrude on the innermost workings of the female anatomy. We are an exterior, surface kind of worker bee. We buzz around the outside of the bush. The other parts—you know, the way inside stuff—is more complicated. We prefer to leave the inner sanctum to you, your partner and occasionally your gynecologist.

The day the girl told me that we had violated her vagina was not accurate. We may have pissed off the skin on her vulva, but we left her actual vagina alone. Did she have an angry kitty when she left? Yeah, she probably did. It was a superficial pissing off though. You see, we prefer a surface cleaning, if you may. We are not in the business of providing a deep, move-the-furniture kind of spring clean. That is beyond our expertise.

We have also learned more about the male anatomy over the past couple years than we ever thought we would. Sleeping with a guy is way different than waxing his parts. We wax a man who had abdominal surgery a few years ago. Unfortunately, the surgery led to some neuropathy in various parts of his body. Neuropathy, for those of you who haven't heard that term before, is a fancy word for nerve damage.

Since some of the nerve damage affected his penis, there are positive and negative ramifications from the neuropathy in that particular area. On a positive note, he doesn't find the process of waxing objectionable. He doesn't complain that it hurts, and he carries on conversations like we're sitting at a bar having a beer. I think he'd prefer being at a bar with us than naked on our table, but that is neither here nor there. The negative part, from our perspective, is that he doesn't have full control of the emissions that leave his body.

One day while we were waxing this particular gentleman, ME noticed that her forearm got wet. She looked up at the ceiling to see if anything was leaking. It's impossible for anything to leak from the ceiling because there's no plumbing directly above the wax room. Even if it were raining cats and dogs, which it wasn't, it would be impossible for any rainwater to drip from the ceiling. There is a third floor that of the salon that is also used for waxing. ME kept looking up and around because she couldn't figure out how her arm could possibly have gotten water on it. Then she looked back down and saw that his penis was leaking. In fact, every time she moved his penis from one side to the other, fluid came out. She wasn't grossed out because she knew that he had no control of this part of his body, so she just wiped it off and finished the job. There was that little part of my brain that imagined the absolute worst-case scenario. It was hard not to get a visual of ME showering in urine. It added some levity to the scenario.

For the record, his penis doesn't leak every time we wax him, but it does happen now and again. We can't wax over an area that is wet, so we make sure to wipe off any parts that get wet while we move his penis from side to side. It really isn't a big deal, and ME has never said anything to him because that could be embarrassing, and she could never hurt his feelings that way. In all honesty, we can't say that his predicament even bothers her anymore. Our bodies change as we age, and his situation is completely out of his control.

She knows that her body has changed a lot as she has entered her fifth decade, and she'd hate for someone to refuse service to her because of a

FIRE
CHIEF

situation she couldn't control. So we just do our job as usual and try to find humor in the situation. We figured that the best way to make it comical was to turn it into an illustration.

There was another leakage problem with a male client that ME found kind of interesting. Of course she did. This particular man suffers from erectile dysfunction. Basically, it means that he can't always maintain an erection, and it can be difficult for him to ejaculate. It's a common problem among men, and it can be emasculating.

Since this client can't ejaculate properly, seminal fluid must get trapped in the shaft of his penis, because when she manipulated his member, sticky ejaculate leaked from the tip. She can't say that it grossed her out or made her uncomfortable. If anything, it made her feel sad for him and for his wife.

Some men with erectile dysfunction use a pump to help them get erect. If they have hair on the shaft of their penis, the hair gets tangled and pulls, and, subsequently, it hurts, which makes it even harder to get an erection. This is why they need people like us. They need to get rid of their hair so they can pump it up with no pain. I'm thinking we could turn this into a song or a poem at least.

Leaky penises are not the only time we have to deal with issues out of the client's control. We've seen other strange things come out of women's bodies as well. Pregnancy is a perfect example. Believe it or not, there are a lot of things we need to take into consideration when we wax women who are in their third trimester of their pregnancy. Things are a lot more complicated with the weight gain, excess blood flow, and stretched-out skin. The waxing service tends to be more risky. That doesn't mean a woman shouldn't do it. If the technician is careful and knows what she's doing, it can be totally safe.

One day, we waxed a woman in her thirty-ninth week. She said that she couldn't lie on her back. We understand that can be a problem when you're pregnant, so we have learned how to position women on one hip, and then the other. What actually happens (here comes the science) is that the uterus slows the circulation in the legs as the baby continues to grow. This can cause a compression of the inferior vena cava, which slows blood flow to the heart.

When the vena cava is compressed, problems can arise. The compression causes women to get dizzy and, sometimes, even pass out.

Even being tilted on one hip was too much for this particular client. As we chatted, we noticed that a wave of white cascaded over her face in a split second. It was the freakiest thing. One minute, we were chatting incessantly, and the next minute, we could tell that all coherent thought had left the building. It was scary. We would hate to do anything that would harm a pregnant mommy or her baby.

ME was scared shitless. The client said she felt faint and needed to reposition her body. We have learned over the years that it is best to turn pregnant women on their left sides when they feel faint, so that's exactly what we did. ME asked her if she needed water. She said yes, provided that ME didn't leave the room to get it. ME used the intercom to ask one of the staff members to bring a glass of water.

After the client drank the water and the color came back to her face, ME was able to finish the entire wax with the woman lying on her side. For a moment, it was nerve wracking, but we made it through it. It was pretty tricky waxing her whole bikini area with her lying on her left side, but we were able to do it. Wax technicians need to accept the fact from the beginning that not everybody can lie or bend the same way.

We have many clients who are inflexible or have injuries that prevent them from assuming the positions that we like to put them into. We are happy to say that our lady who was about to pass out went on to have a healthy baby the following week.

Since we're talking about pregnant women, we have to say that we have come across a lot more women who pass their mucous plugs on the table. For those of you who don't know what we are talking about, the mucous plug lives way up high in the cervical area when you are pregnant. As you get ready to have that precious little bambino, the plug (or glob of mucus) exits your body. It can trickle out or pass as one big clump of slime. This may not sound scientific, but it's exactly what it looks like. We don't know if it's because ME has had children or that she has become immune to gross shit over the years, but seeing the mucous between a woman's legs really doesn't gross her out anymore. We know what it is. We just clean up the area as we do our thing and know that the client is one step closer to having a baby.

We explained the whole mucus plug thing to our staff. They needed to know what it was all about since they've never had kids themselves. They were a little freaked out about it at first, but it was the perfect time for educate them. This is part of what we told them. If a pregnant woman comes in and she has an unusual discharge, don't be alarmed or grossed out because it just means she is one step closer to having a baby. If a woman who is not pregnant has some weird discharge, be annoyed because that is just not OK. Then you should plaster a big smile on your face and try not to vomit on said client.

Pregnant talk reminds us of a funny story that happened with one of our baby doctors that we wax. One day, an obstetrician in her early thirties came in for a Brazilian. She was the biggest pansy. She needed breaks. She complained about the pain and kept asking us to stop. She didn't want us to finish. It was pretty pathetic. During one of our very short breaks, ME (who hates being told to slow down and wait) told the OB in a domineering voice, "The next time you give someone a uterine biopsy, think of me, because this Brazilian thing ain't nothing compared to one of those!"

The OB wasn't quite sure how to respond to that. We discovered that she never had a uterine biopsy, but we assured her that a Brazilian was a cakewalk in comparison. She understood the analogy and tried to stop whining.

The next day, she sent ME an e-mail apologizing for being such a weanie. She promised to do better next time (like there would be a next time). She said she was happy that we persevered and finished the service, because she loved her wax. We had to laugh because most technicians would have given up and just let her leave the salon unfinished. But we couldn't do that. It doesn't take long to wax someone, and we knew if we finished the service, she would be happy. She was.

About two months later, she actually came back. We really didn't think she would. One of the first things she said was that not only did she love having a Brazilian, but so did her husband. In fact, she told us that he couldn't keep his face out of our work. That admission makes us so happy. She felt amazing. Her sex life had improved like she could have never imagined. In fact, she said that she hadn't had that much sex since they were first married.

Go ME! How many times do we have to tell people that their sex lives will improve when they start waxing? This woman discovered that all the pain and agony she endured was more than worth it. We knew it would be if she let us finish. Yes, it would have been much easier to let her leave, but we couldn't do that. We can't leave a job half done.

Her hair wasn't that coarse, and she was a slender and fit person. We knew we could have her done in less than ten minutes if she would let us do our job. This time, she did. She was proud of herself and very happy. The Happy Hoo-Ha strikes again!

Speaking of husbands not being able to keep their faces out of bald pussies...A woman told me her husband called her as she was driving to the salon. He wanted to know if she was on her way home. She told him she was on her way to see ME first. His immediate response was that he wished he could breathe out of his ears. That is a definite superpower that I think a lot of men wish they could possess.

Isn't this chapter supposed to be about science or some kind of shit like that? How come we always end up talking about sex? OK then, let's get back to some science and a woman's anatomy. When something unusual appears on your body (like some kind of growth or a strange-looking mark), you don't always know what it is. Some people find weird growths on their bodies and freak out and expect the worse. Others don't pay much attention and hope they goes away. It is not as uncommon as you might think for women to confuse ingrown hairs with herpes. It's an honest mistake, and we would never mock someone out for being overzealous about their sexual health. It's one of our most favorite areas, and we believe it should be kept clean, bald, and healthy. We've even had multiple clients tell us that they went to the doctor to be tested for herpes just to be on the safe side. In most cases, the threat of herpes turns out to be a stubborn ingrown hair.

We just wanted to let you know that most people get ingrown hairs from time to time. Some get a lot. Some people get a random one here and there. You can get ingrown hairs whether you shave, wax, or do nothing.

The problem, as we see it, is now that more people get Brazilians, the ingrown hairs are more obvious because there is no hair covering the pubic area. You may not have ever known you had ingrown hairs if you were sporting that seventies bush. We don't know how anyone can expect to see anything that is happening beneath that Afro that you need to blow-dry when you get out of the shower. Now that you've gotten a Brazilian and you're bald, voilà, there they are. Don't freak out when you see those stubborn little hairs that get trapped beneath your skin. Almost everyone gets an ingrown hair from time to time, and some people get a whole family of them. It just depends on your hair, your skin, and how you maintain that area. It isn't something to freak out about. The chance of them getting infected is pretty low.

The positive part of this commentary is that most people get fewer ingrown hairs from waxing than shaving. Moreover, when you wax, your hair comes in finer and thinner, so it's usually easier to get those buggers out. A nice pair of pointy tweezers works wonders at extracting those bad boys. It's just another advantage to waxing it all.

Fortunately, ingrown hairs are usually harmless and tend to not have any odor. If they do contain an odor, there is always the possibility that the hair has developed an abscess and will need to be surgically cleaned out. Having a doctor lance an abscess isn't the end of the world, but it can leave a scar, in case you were wondering.

In most cases, an unpleasant smell has nothing to do with a stubborn hair that doesn't want to grow out of the skin properly. It has to do with the shitty job a person does cleaning her snatch. Therefore, we are thinking about inventing a device that we can use when we wax someone smelly. Watch out NASA. ME is becoming an inventor.

Now that we are older, we have to wear eyeglasses all the time. Since we already have something attached to our faces all day long, we've come up with this brilliant idea. We'd like to invent a set of glasses with two small fans attached on either side to push any unpleasant odor away from ME. The clever part of this is that the odor would be focused in the direction of the client. This way, maybe the client would understand how stinky her snatch is and think twice about getting waxed when her lady parts are not in the most pristine condition.

We're still working on what to call this clever invention. We're thinking about maybe a Brazilian blow torch. Fumes are like flames in ME's mind. This illustration demonstrates how the contraption would work. The first time ME wrote that sentence, she wrote *contraception* instead of *contraption.* I'm not sure, but I think that could be called a Freudian slip. If you think about it, if someone really smells, the odor would be a great form of birth control.

One day, two psychologists came in for waxes. Sometimes we can figure out what people do for a living just by the way they act, the things they say, or the questions they ask. These ladies kept telling each other to go to their "safe place." The way they talked to each other sounded like the way a psychologist would talk to you. It sounded comforting and placating. We like to tell people to go their happy place, but the safe place works too. We don't think their safe place worked for them, because they didn't come back.

We think the whole waxing thing actually traumatized these ladies. The one was completely convinced that nothing should be put so far "in there." Her anxiety about the extent of our thoroughness was unnecessary. For the record, we don't really go in anywhere besides the creases. It may appear that we are going into unchartered territories with our craft sticks, but, believe me, we know the difference between the surface area and the internal forbidden fruit. We are cautious to not go inside any parts between the legs or butt cheeks. As mentioned earlier, the inner sanctums are for physicians and lovers. Period. And occasionally for tampons and dildos.

The number of different coping mechanisms they tried during such a short amount of time was incredible. When the quest to go to the safe place didn't work, they started reciting YouTube videos. We weren't sure what they were talking about at first, but then they explained it. They have watched a particular YouTube video many times. When they need a good laugh, they recite the conversation from the video. This is what they did to distract themselves from the pain. We didn't understand the reference and had never seen the video they were talking about, so we just went with it, and it was

impossible not to laugh with them. They were the comediennes during this exchange.

ME has worked diligently over the years to perfect her service. She thinks Brazilian bikini waxing is one of the most important grooming habits that women need to do. However, she is not a huge fan of bikini waxing. Bikini waxing refers to the sides of the pubis and a little bit on the top of the thigh. In her opinion, labia and rectal hair can be gross and needs to go. That's why when you come to her for a bikini wax, nine times out of ten, you'll leave with a Brazilian.

So how does she manage that? Science, baby. She asks the client to remove her underwear on the pretense that she doesn't want to get any wax on it, which she doesn't. It's also easier to tell whether or not she is being symmetrical when she leaves a shape behind. It isn't the main reason though. Asking a client to remove her undies is part of the ploy to get them to "waxitall" just like her license plate reads. Then, as she is working hard to distract the client, she asks what the objection to removing the lip and ass hair is. Pain is the number one reason. Usually, by this point in the service, she is one rip away from removing all of the lip hair on one side of the person's body. Next thing you know, she has skinned the kitty! It has taken her years to perfect this technique, but it works like a charm.

Women often get possessed when they are getting a wax. I think it goes back to the whole fight-or-flight response. The following scene was so funny that we decided to call it "The Sybil Effect." I think scientists would have a ball with this one.

This particular client needed to talk to herself in order to muster the courage to endure the grueling seven-minute service. We wrote down the exchange as soon as we finished waxing her, so we wouldn't forget what she said. We think we got it just about perfect.

She started out by saying, "I'm a bad ass."

A minute later, she said, "Oh fuck."

Another minute passed, and she said, "This doesn't hurt."

A moment passed, and she said with more emotion, "Holy shit!"

A second later, she said, "No, I am a bad ass."

Her final words were, "Oh fuck, no I'm not!"

Maybe ME and I aren't scientists, but we definitely scrutinize the procedures and techniques that we use to ensure that every client gets the best wax possible. We do believe in the science behind the art of waxing. It is most definitely an art. Nothing, in our opinion, is most beautiful than a perfectly primped pussy.

Jack-in-the-Box

In That Happy Hoo-Ha, ME wrote a chapter about men called "Guys are the Real Pussies." She didn't mean any disrespect by the name, but at that point in her career, only men had passed out on her, so the name was pretty fitting. One guy passed out from getting his nipples waxed. That was pretty pathetic. The second man passed out from getting his back waxed. Still pretty lame.

During that time, ME had decided not to wax men's genitalia for a variety of reasons. The scrotum has pretty thin skin that can tear, which is nerve wracking. We also got a lot of calls from perverts, and she didn't want to deal with assholes getting excited because she was touching their junk. Believe me, there are some sick fucks out there.

After the first book was finished, she started on the second book right away. There was such a legitimate demand at the time for men's Brazilians that she decided it was time to bite the bullet (not men's little bullets) and start doing them again. It was funny, because once she said she would start waxing men again, the calls began to wane. All of a sudden, men weren't feeling as brave about asking for an appointment as they were before she agreed to do them. (Don't you mean wax them?)

Waxing a man's private parts is such a different experience that she decided to add a chapter in the second book called "Got 'Em by the Balls." We still have to worry about pissing off their scrotums, but most men think it's worth it. And if they pull any shit on ME, she has gotten so much more brazen as she has gotten older that we promise they will regret their inappropriateness.

Now she has a lot more experience waxing men. Since she mostly waxes women, it's a nice diversion doing a guy once in a while. We never had any intention of devoting an entire chapter to men again, but there were enough stories to make it worth our while and hopefully to make you laugh.

If you're wondering about the title of this chapter, you'll have to wait until the end of it to see what it means. Once you've read about a few of ME's experiences, you may be able to figure out how we came up with the name. If don't want to think that hard and just wait until the end, that's good too.

We'd like to preface this chapter with a funny story about one of ME's employees. When ME started doing Brazilians on men, she asked a senior staff member if she was interested in learning how to wax the private parts of men. The staff member said that she didn't feel comfortable doing it, which was fine with us. We'd never want her to do anything that made her uncomfortable. Not only would the client sense the staff member's unease, it could make her not want to work at Mark & M. E., and, at the time, she was too valuable to lose. Since we started this book, she decided to leave anyway, but that's not the fun part of this story.

A few months later, we hired a spunky young woman who had worked at a men's hair salon for four years. She seemed to be comfortable working with men. After a few months doing hair and nails at the salon, it was time for us to start training her to wax. She seemed to catch on to our technique fairly quickly and we felt that she could be a real asset to us in the wax room as well.

One day, ME asked to speak with her privately. She instantly looked nervous, like she thought she was going to be criticized for something she did wrong. Although we had already observed that she took constructive criticism better than any employee we ever had, we didn't have anything critical to talk to her about. It was still kind of funny to watch her squirm though. Our need to speak with her was about her interest in learning to do new things at Mark & M. E. More specifically, we needed to know how she would feel about working on men's private areas.

ME looked at her seriously and with literally no affect in her voice or on her face, she asked her how she felt about penises. Without missing a beat, the staff member said that she liked them inside her. You must love a clever and witty response like that! Believe me, that's the kind of person you want doing Brazilians. You want someone who is quick, funny, and outgoing. She continued by asking ME if that was her way of finding out if she was a lesbian or not. We had to laugh, because we couldn't have cared less if she was gay.

ME explained that she wanted to know how she felt about performing a men's Brazilian. She told us she preferred working on men since most of her salon experience was with them. She was also psyched to learn how to do more things at the salon. Then we both started laughing hysterically. It was the strangest and funniest exchange.

During her initial interview for a job at Mark & M.E., she told ME that she was a little star struck meeting her. ME had no idea what she was talking about. Apparently, this prospective employee read *The Happy Hoo-Ha* and thought ME was funny, so she started following her on all of her social-media sites. When her sister saw that we were hiring, she reread the book before the interview. Since then, she told us that she was determined to be in the next book. We don't know if she suspects that our penis discussion was what gave her the distinction to be in *The Happy Trail*, but we thought it was a perfect way to get her in here, because it was funny as shit.

Since we started this book, this new girl has taken on the role of ripping men seriously but with a great deal of humor. To us, that is the perfect combination. Make them laugh while you're ripping their junk. It's obvious that she likes talking to the men and, for some reason, finds their parts less intimidating then vaginas. Whatever works. She has been a tremendous asset to our team.

One day, when she finished giving a man a Brazilian, we asked her how the wax went. She said it didn't go well. It appears that when she lifted up the man's testicles, the area underneath was dirty. She had never experienced that before and was pretty grossed out by it, which is completely understandable. Unfortunately, dirty body parts are one of the side effects of waxing private regions. Everyone deals with adversity differently, and we have explained to our staff that they have to be able to stomach nasty shit (pun intended) or the whole waxing gig won't work for them.

The next day, I told her we had a present for her. She opened up an envelope that had two Hershey's Kisses in it. We thought two was an appropriate number for the area in question. We also had a card in there. The card congratulated her for truly being initiated into the Mark & M. E. family. You can't be a real wax technician if don't experience some gross shit once in a while. We also told her that she would never look at chocolate the same way again. We're not sure if she ate the Kisses.

Most people assume that all men who get Brazilians are gay, but that is not our experience. In fact, we don't wax many gay men at all. One day, a handsome college student came in for a wax. We had a feeling he might be gay, but we couldn't have cared less one way or the other.

It was obvious that he used clippers on his chest. In fact, he trimmed the hair on his chest really short. Meanwhile, we were focused on making his midsection completely bald. His leg hair, on the other hand, was extremely long. We recommended that he use the clippers on his legs as well, because his hair was so long and dense, and it looked a little funny in contrast to the rest of his body. ME suggested that he not cut the hair as short as his chest, but she thought it would look good if he trimmed it down some. If he left it a little longer, it wouldn't be so stubbly. That's when he blurted out, "I'm gay, you know!" Yep, you got it. He thought ME was hitting on him.

Maybe if she wasn't so opinionated and hadn't shared her opinion on his leg hair, she wouldn't have scared the poor boy. She has been married throughout her entire salon career, so she has never had the inclination to hit on anyone. She especially wouldn't be interested in a man in his early twenties. He must have thought she was a cougar who prayed on cute, young men. That couldn't have been further from the truth. She just wanted to offer a constructive grooming suggestion.

It's hard not to offer advice about grooming options for dealing with body hair, because a lot of men don't realize they can clipper cut hair on any part of their bodies. For example, many men have never entertained the thought of trimming the hair under their arms. Not only does it reduce the sweat and potential odor, it makes deodorant go on more smoothly.

ME deals in hair all day, and she tries to be as helpful as possible. She felt badly that this kid thought she was hitting on him. It was never her intent. He was her son's age, for God's sake.

He seemed a little uncomfortable after that, so she assured him that she was happily married to Mark. She furthered by telling him that they had been together for thirty years. She also told him that she had two children who were older then he was. She finished off by telling him that she was more than twice his age and was just offering a suggestion. It's really strange trying to justify your comments when they are totally misconstrued. I think she made her point as best as she could. The whole thing was just weird.

On the other end of the spectrum is our more mature male clientele. To date, our oldest male client who gets a Brazilian is seventy years old. One day we noticed he had a backpack with him. We asked him if he had gone to school that day. He laughed and said that walking up the flight of stairs to the second floor of our salon last time winded him, so he brought his oxygen tank with him. He didn't bring it with him the first time, so, for a moment, we couldn't help but feel grateful that the pain of the wax didn't make him hyperventilate or wheeze during our first encounter. It was just our flight of stairs that knocked him out.

When we entered the wax room, he told us that he put a breath mint in his mouth to cover up the cigarette smell. He continued by saying that after he did that, he realized that we wouldn't be near that part of his body so it really wouldn't matter. That's when we realized that he was a smoker with an oxygen tank! Believe me, we couldn't have cared less about his cigarette breath. We just wanted to make sure he didn't blow himself or the salon up! OK, maybe ME was a little more concerned about the salon blowing up. In her defense, she does have college tuition bills to pay.

She threatened him a little. She told him that she had two kids in college and couldn't risk having the place blown up. He thought that was funny—like her comment was absurd. There's nothing absurd about fire and oxygen. She also asked him how his pulmonary doctor felt about his smoking. He just laughed.

He's actually a pretty funny guy, and we have had some interesting conversations. ME knew he was married, so she asked him if his wife would be interested in getting waxed. He scoffed and said there was no way she would do it. In fact, she thought he was strange for getting it done. As the conversation continued, he told ME that he needed a girlfriend. She asked him why, since he already had a wife. He told her that the only thing his wife liked to do was iron. And then he repeated it once again so that she fully understood that the only thing his wife liked to do was iron. Think he was hitting on our girl?

She had to change the topic after that, because it was obvious he found her appealing, and she didn't want any spontaneous eruptions on the table. She needed to remind him that she was a professional who was just doing a job that she did all day long. As it turns out, they found plenty of other things to talk about.

So let's talk about the spontaneous eruption that we alluded to. When we started *The Happy Trail* in 2014, we had marked over twenty years in this business and had never had a man ejaculate during a service at the salon in front of ME or any of her staff members. But now it's 2015, and we can say that our jizz-free state is officially over.

We have two women who currently wax at the salon. When my spunky girl waxed "The Ejaculator" (that's what we call him), he had an erection the entire time. He went as far as to grab his cock and wave it at her. She remained professional and finished the service as efficiently as possible. Erections are not uncommon, so we just muddle through the service as though it means nothing, which it usually doesn't.

But The Ejaculator was enjoying this more than he should have. Our second wax technician entered the room to wax his buttocks. She is a beautiful young woman who is new to the business. Yep, we gave the creeper to the new girl. In fact, she had only been working for us for about six weeks, but she exhibited quite an aptitude for waxing from the get-go. And boy, did he let go.

When a man gets his butt waxed, we have him lying on his stomach. Before this client got up, he informed our employee that he just came on the table. And he did.

We posted the occurrence on Facebook, and our followers were outraged. We have dozens of people in the salon business who follow our posts, so we thought it was important to let them know that this absolutely unacceptable thing happened. Many suggested we call the police and report it. We didn't. We just decided not to service him anymore. (OK, that sounded a little like someone from a brothel talking.)

Ironically, a few weeks later, he came back to the salon and apologized profusely for his behavior. It appears that he follows us on Facebook and saw the numerous suggestions to contact the authorities. We're not convinced that he was genuinely sorry. We think he was more afraid that we would call the cops and was hoping that we wouldn't if he apologized.

Jizz

If you jizz on my table,
You know what I'll do?
Leave wax on your balls
That will stick like glue.
It'll take weeks for the wax
To fully go away,
And your balls will be raw
For day after day.
If you get horny,
We do understand,
Think of something nasty,
And act like a man.
You're no longer a teen
With no more control;
We may still call the cops
And put you on parole.
If you jizz on my table—
You know, I'm serious—
Your balls will hurt so bad
You'll be rendered delirious.

The incident with The Ejaculator was an isolated occurrance. Most men legitimately want their junk waxed, and we have no problem making them as bald as their female counterparts.

The following story is one of our favorites. A forty-year-old guy came in for a Brazilian. He was pretty tall. In fact, his feet hung over the end of the table. He was married, was tired of shaving, and thought his wife would like it if he got waxed. He was fair skinned, and fair-skinned people tend to be more sensitive. His hair was pretty prickly from shaving, and we knew that would make his hair more stubborn to remove. To make matters worse, much of his pubic hair was gray. Gray hair can be a bitch to rip out sometimes. We tried hard to keep him distracted with animated stories, and we did a pretty good job keeping him engaged in conversation. Still, we could tell he was in a lot of pain. He squirmed a lot on the table, and ME asked him if he wanted her to stop, because he kept pulling away from her. He said that he wanted her to finish even though he was dying and it totally sucked.

While ME waxed the shaft of his penis, she had a pretty tight hold on the end of it. She has learned that it's important to hold it tight. When she ripped a strip of hair off, his entire torso slid off the table. That was taking the whole squirm thing to an extreme.

The best part of the story is that as he slipped off the table, she didn't let go of his penis. She didn't want him falling off the table, because he could have gotten hurt. Even though this was the first time she had met him, she said quite emphatically, "Hey, where the fuck do you think you're going?"

His story is not over. Once she got him situated back on the table, fixed the, pillow and straightened the bed sheets, she asked him if he wanted her to finish. He said that he did. So she continued on her journey through his Brazilian rain forest with as much levity as she could muster. It couldn't have been any more apparent, however, that he was not a happy camper. At one point, she looked at him and said, "Don't forget, you love me!"

He responded by saying that he would love her forever if she told him that this was the last rip. Sadly, it wasn't. There were a few sections left. When ME sent that story to her illustrator, he sent her an email back saying that he and his wife kept laughing at the sentence when ME said, "Where the fuck do you thing you're going?" She seriously was not letting go.

Robbins 2015

It shouldn't come as a surprise to you that the biggest question we get from both men and women is whether or not men get erections when they get Brazilians. In most cases, no matter how hard up a man may be, his bad boy shrinks into an abyss once you start waxing. But there are definitely some exceptions.

A guy in his twenties came in one day for his first-ever Brazilian wax. He wasn't very tall, and he was pretty slender. When he removed his slacks, he had quite an erection protruding from the bottom of his dress shirt. It was a fairly decent size appendage compared to the size of his body. Our girl turned away from him so he wouldn't be embarrassed and started putting her gloves on. While she had her back to him, she told him to lie down and face the sky. We have a beautiful light above the table that looks like a tree and the sky. When she turned back to face him, his cock was literally facing the sky. We're not sure he noticed the irony in her expression, but we sure did.

Unfortunately, he didn't have any pubic hair on the side of the bikini line. The only hair he had in that area surrounded his penis like long, thick sea grass. Since she couldn't start on the side of his erection where his bikini line would normally be, she had no choice but to dig right in. She usually flops the penis from one side to the other to wax the front of the bikini area, but there was no flopping this one. She tried, but it wasn't going anywhere. She had to come up with another approach. So she bent his leg, lifted up the side of his scrotum, and removed hair from one of the most sensitive spots in that region.

Starting in this area seemed to do the trick. He got smaller after the first rip. By the third rip, we both swear we heard his cock shrivel down to a little cigar nub. It almost sounded like a balloon deflating. We wish there was some way we could describe to you how it sounded in our heads, even though there probably wasn't any sound at all.

Honestly, it was satisfying to see it get smaller. He didn't apologize for having an erection or say anything at all, which made it awkward, to say the least.

We have definitely concluded that some men get erections when they're nervous. We just would have appreciated a heads-up (good one) that it was a "nervous" boner and not a "holy shit, you're a hot lady" boner.

ME didn't really think he found her so alluring that his parts felt the need to salute her, but you never know. In case he did like older women and the arousal was misguided and inappropriate, she asked him how old he was. When he said he was twenty-five years old, she mentioned that she was twice his age. When that didn't seem to do the trick, she also commented on how she was married to Mark and had been for nearly thirty years. Sadly, the only thing that made it relax was the excruciating pain he was in.

The second time he came in, she knew exactly who he was because the same thing happened again. She even took him into a different room, hoping that a change in scenery would make a difference. Wrong. Once again, he had a full-fledged erection when he removed his pants, and, once again, it took a few rips to make it go down. This is when she realized that there had to be a correlation between his nerves and his erection, and she felt confident that he had no control over the situation.

If you had any desire to hear her tell the story of the "erection guy," as we like to refer to him at Mark & M. E., please check out her first ever stand-up on YouTube. Just type in "the Happy Hoo-Ha Live," and you can hear her tell the entire story.

You must be wondering why the hell men and women subject themselves to this kind of pubic torture. The best answer we can give you is that it is worth it. If it wasn't, there wouldn't be so many people getting it done.

One night we got a Facebook message from a female client who said that her husband had lost a bet and had to get a Brazilian. They came in a few days later so that ME could wax both of them. During the service, she asked them if they would tell her what they bet on. She prefaced by saying that if it was too personal, they didn't have to tell her.

The wife told her that one night they got really drunk, made a bet, and sent us a message about him getting waxed since he lost. The following morning, she vaguely remembered the bet and checked her Facebook page to see if she really sent us a message. Although she remembered sending the message, she absolutely could not remember what they bet on. Funny thing is that he had no idea either. He sort of remembered that he agreed to getting waxed. He also figured that if she sent a message, then he must have really lost whatever bet they had made. Gotta love a man who stands by his word even when he can't remember what that word is!

As you can see, adding men into the equation has been quite amusing. It adds a whole other dimension to ME's day. It's funny because we're used to seeing piercings on women, but is has been pretty interesting to see the piercings on the guys. One of the guys ME waxed had a really large and thick silver ring at the end of his penis. Fortunately, it didn't get in the way, because there was no hair at that end. If there were hair on that part, we would have both freaked out.

When she moved his penis from one side to the other, she couldn't believe how heavy the piercing was. She had two questions she wanted to ask him, but she didn't. Blows my mind how sometimes ME will ask the craziest shit, and, other times, she is shy about what she asks people. She was planning to ask him questions about his piercing the next time he came in, but that never happened. She was actually surprised he didn't come back. If you can handle getting a big hole put in the tip of your cock, we don't understand why you can't handle a Brazilian.

Her first question would have been, "Has your penis gotten longer since you've been wearing that piercing?" I imagine it had to because that sucker was freaking heavy. The second question was whether or not his wife made him take it out when they had sex, because it looked like it would hurt. She was not sure her body would have enjoyed that bad boy jamming in her.

All I can say is that inquiring minds wanted to know, but she was too shy to ask. There's a first for everything.

Occasionally some clients refer to themselves in the third person. In order to share this story effectively, we are going to make up a name for this man so we can better describe what transpired during his service. Let's call him Richard Weiner (no, he's not related to Dick Head). As ME was waxing his junk, he loudly exclaimed, "You got this Weiner. Can't believe you're doing this, Weiner. So proud of you, Weiner." It sounded a little peculiar to ME the first time he said it, but he continued to talk to himself that way through the whole service.

She started thinking about it more seriously and began to wonder why he would speak about himself in the third person. This is what she came up with. (ME, the self-appointed psychiatrist, is at it again.) She thinks it was his way of coping with the pain that she was inflicting upon him. She also thinks it may have been a way for him to remove himself from any awkwardness he might have felt getting this done for the first time. Both reasons seemed plausible, so she just went with it. She assumed that the next time he came in, he would feel more comfortable and not feel the need to refer to himself in the same way. Well, the second time he came in, he was still talking to Weiner again. I guess he just likes talking to his little wiener.

Unless a man is paralyzed below the waist, there will be some discomfort when he gets a wax. It isn't a pleasant experience, and the skin on the scrotum is thin and delicate. We have had a few men start to grow when we touch their penises, but as soon as we wax any of the area, their penises go right back where they belong. Hidden in their shells like the heads of turtles hiding in theirs.

Speaking of turtles (one thought always seems to lead to the next...), I have been surprised by how many men come into the salon who haven't been circumcised. One of the guys ME waxes on a regular basis wanted to know if she waxed a lot of uncircumcised men. She was glad that he asked her that, because she didn't realize how many men weren't. In fact, she was so psyched that he mentioned it, because it really kind of baffled her—not only how many uncircumcised men she had met, but if there was a reason it was so popular to get waxed in that population.

He asked her if she wanted to know why it was so important not to have hair on the shaft of the penis for men who still have their foreskin. Of course we wanted to know! We wanted to know as much detail as possible about everything that has to do with penises, vaginas, sex...

Apparently, when an uncircumcised penis loses an erection, the hair on the shaft gets tangled in the tip and can be uncomfortable. He said it feels like someone is pulling his pubic hair, and it can really hurt. Well, that kind of sucks for our non-metrosexual, uncircumcised dudes out there who don't groom their junk. It shouldn't surprise you that we found this bit of information quite fascinating, and we were excited to share it with you. It must be the teacher part of our personality that always wants to educate. You have to admit that this subject matter is way more fascinating than high school earth science.

It is a little trickier to wax an uncut cock. (We had to try out how that sounded) C'mon, Reader, please say it aloud for me. Uncut cock. It's fun to say, don't you think? Naturally ME wrote a poem about an uncircumcised man whom she found quite difficult to wax. We'd like to introduce you to the man with the slippery slinky.

Slippery Slinky

Some things about my job
Are harder than others—
Like the natural state
Of some of the brothers

Who haven't been cut
In the hospital at birth
And can brag about more length
Than the actual girth.

It's the way that all men
Come into our world,
Which some find erotic
And others absurd.

I couldn't care less
If you have extra skin;
I'll still make you bald.
To be bare is to win.

But that extra flap of skin
Makes it more complicated,
Since the pain makes it soft
And utterly deflated.

Holding it tight
To wax off the hair
Is tricky at best.
As I strive to make it bare,

I try to hang on
To your soft little winky,
But it likes to collapse
Like a slippery slinky.

I know that it's better
With no hair on the shaft;
You can work so much harder
To hone your sex craft.

If there's hair left behind
When the member is big,
The climax and descent
Is an uncomfortable gig.

I do my best
To be thorough and good,
So hard or soft
You have the best hunk of wood.

Fortunately, this man has no idea how difficult it is for ME to wax him. The more she does it, the easier it becomes. She just has to try different techniques to hold his parts in ways that will help her wax him more efficiently. He is in his fifties and decided to start waxing on a regular basis upon hitting that half-a-century mark. He told her that it hasn't been easy for him to work monthly Brazilians into his budget, but he has made them a priority and has made changes to his other expenses to make it work. What cemented his decision to wax on a regular basis has to do with his casual encounters through online dating. He told her he has gotten compliments on how soft his balls are, and a few women have asked what he does to get them so soft. He is proud to say he gets waxed on a regular basis. And he should be. We applaud his commitment and dedication not only to us but to the waxing as well.

Women have been coming to Mark & M.E. for years to get waxed, because getting a Brazilian was one of the items on their "bucket lists." We can now officially say that men have told us the same thing. One man had a pretty decent bucket list that he wanted to complete before his fortieth birthday. The first time he came to us for a Brazilian was a few months before the big four-oh. He did well, loved the results, and is now a regular client. More importantly, his wife loves how soft his skin is without any hair on it, and she appreciates how thorough a job we do. More often than not, bucket-list people get so worked up about the anticipated pain that they aren't cooperative during the service and tend to not be repeat customers.

We love that men of all ages are paying more attention to their personal grooming. Clients have asked about hair from their ears to their feet. A few of the men we wax don't have any chest hair, but they do have random stringy hairs around their nipples. It's easy to wax the nipples, and you shouldn't be afraid to get it done. All you have to do is ask. We don't judge. We just love ripping out hair, and we want you to feel good about your body.

Don't be alarmed if you read ME's first book and you come across the incident where she talks about the nipple guy. There is a chapter in *The Happy Hoo-Ha* called "Guys Are the Real Pussies," where she talks about a guy who had a few stringy nipple hairs on them that she waxed for him Sadly, he passed out on the table. But that was a one-time occurrence, and no men have passed out from getting their nipples waxed ever since.

As a guy, I'm not sure I feel much better after you mentioned the whole passing-out thing. Is that like saying it's safe to bungee jump even though X number of people have crashed headfirst onto the ground and died instantly?

We have discovered that the radio is really a great way to get our name out there. A local Rochester disc jockey named Brother Wease has been awesome, not only having ME on his show, but also talking about her even when she's not there. One day, a guy who had heard her on the radio came in to get a variety of body parts waxed. He was in the waiting room talking to Mark when ME walked in, said hello, and told him she was ready to take him upstairs. He looked at her with a fairly puzzled expression and said he was shocked that the "famous ME" was going to wax him. OK, famous in her own mind, maybe, but other than that, not so much.

He seemed surprised and was overly enthusiastic that ME would be performing the service on him. She told him that she was the only one who waxed wee-wees in the joint (and, at the time, she was), so he was stuck with her. That was the start of a really fun appointment and a budding relationship.

There are risks to waxing any body part, but some parts are more sensitive than others. The scrotum, for example, is one of those extra-sensitive parts. Surprised? Not only is it tricky to keep the skin taut, but it tends to get irritated. It often looks like a skinned knee where a thin layer of skin has been removed. We have tried several types of wax, and we can never judge whether or not the skin will react badly or not.

ME once tweeted, "Balls make me sweat." They really do. It was funny how many people responded to that Twitter post. One guy commented that getting his balls waxed would make him sweat way harder than she ever could. He had her with that one. From a technician's point of view, we don't want the balls to sweat since hot wax doesn't adhere to wet surfaces, as we mentioned before.

OK, you have got to hear what just happened. ME was writing this part of the book while she and Mark were sitting on a plane in business class with her mom and boyfriend. They were coming back from ME's big fiftieth celebration cruise that went from Turkey to Italy. As she finished writing about the sweaty balls, the flight attendant handed her a small bowl of nuts, which happened to be warm. The timing couldn't have been more perfect. As soon as ME put a nut in her mouth, she couldn't stop laughing about the attendant's impeccable timing. What are the chances that someone would hand her a bowl of warm nuts while she was writing about the exact same thing?

We've also tweeted that sometimes balls bleed. This is one of those details we probably shouldn't have mentioned. We think it may have turned off some potential male wax clients. You think? Unfortunately, there can be some blood involved when you remove hair from the balls, the beaver, or any part of the body, for that matter. Remember poor old Bill?

We have to admit that we've had better luck waxing black men's balls then white men's balls. If you didn't happen to notice the picture on the back of this book, ME is a white woman. She is also a woman who has had limited experience with black men, and, more specifically, with their balls. Well, that's not something you hear every day, I bet. In most cases, she has found that their skin seems to be a little tougher and doesn't tend to get those slight tears in it like their white counterparts. I have to wonder though if she just can't see the tears because things are dark, and her eyesight is rapidly declining. Either way, she always tries to be as careful as possible with that part of the body, but let's face it, she just finished telling you that it is a tough area to hold taut and that skin is stupid sensitive.

In her experience, she has found that oilier skin—which black skin tends to be—seems to get less irritated. We have to admit it is definitely harder to see the hair when everything is dark, but we always try to be as thorough as possible. She often has to look at the hair from several angles to make sure she gets it all, but she does that with blonds as well, so it's not as weird as it seems. OK, maybe it is.

One time, she was waxing a black man with his wife sitting in the room. We encourage spouses to come into the room because it can make the experience so much more entertaining. This wasn't one of those times. The wife just sat there playing on her phone and engaging in conversation, but he seemed really uncomfortable with having his wife in the room.

ME had waxed him several times before, and it never felt weird or awkward until this particular day. We don't think he was comfortable with his wife in the room while another woman removed all the pubic hair on his penis. In fact, it was the first time he sweat during a service with ME. She couldn't help but feel his unease, and that made her feel a little strange as well. Actually, it sucked.

She got to the point where she needed to look at his parts from every angle to make sure she had waxed all the hairs. At this point in the service, if she finds any stray hairs, she tweezes them out. Due to his discomfort, she was nervous about getting her head too close to his body to look for any stray hairs. From the wife's vantage point, the position of ME's head near his midsection could have been misconstrued. ME was sitting at the head of the table, so it could have looked like she was giving him a blow job.

For some reason, ME worried that the wife might freak out. (Admit it, you thought she might hit you.) ME looked at the wife and warned her that she would be putting her right ear near his chest to look at his penis from different angles. She explained that it was difficult to get all the hairs that nestle in the creases, and she wanted to be a thorough as possible. She went on to mention that it's hard to see all the little hairs since his skin and hair were both so dark. Then she said that the husband told her how much his wife liked having all the hair gone down there, and ME wanted to do a really good job. The wife couldn't have cared less. ME was worried for nothing.

There aren't many instances where ME's uncomfortable working on a client. In most cases, there is lots of chatter and, usually, a lot of laughter. In *The Happy Hen House*, she told her readers a story about an older woman who was disappointed that her hair didn't grow faster because she loved hearing the stories. Since that story came out, the client has actually said something similar again. Even telling the story about ME's fear of getting hit by a jealous wife has some comedic value to it.

ME is proud to announce that a man told her he looked forward to coming back because she made him laugh so hard during his appointment. That made ME really happy. She appreciated his feedback and was glad he enjoyed his service with her. In fact, it was a pretty neat compliment that made her day. Since she never aspired to be a comedienne, it's exciting for her to know she has the ability to make people laugh. Sure as hell beats making the clients cry.

Since this is a chapter dedicated to men, it's time to get back to the sac. They say that men's voices can get higher when they're kicked in the balls, but what about when you wax them in that area? We finally experienced a heterosexual, forty-year-old guy losing control of the deep octave range that normally resonates from his vocal chords. He actually squealed; I want to say like a girl, but it was more like a mouse. ME and his girlfriend couldn't stop laughing because it was such a foreign sound coming out of his mouth.

Mock a guy in pain. Nice job, ladies.

The girlfriend snorted and said, "What the hell was that sound?"

He didn't even notice that they were laughing at him because he found the experience more painful than he ever imagined. Furthermore, neither of them could mimic him, because their voices couldn't get that high.

When you're in pain, your adrenaline kicks in, and what can happen to the body can be freaky. Sometimes the adrenaline causes a person's limbs to shake uncontrollably. We have gotten used to shaky body parts, and it doesn't bother us in the least because we've seen it happen to countless clients over the years. Although it can be distracting, it usually doesn't get in the way or stop us from doing our jobs.

One time we were waxing a man, and his leg trembled badly. He apologized and was very embarrassed. We told him that there was no reason to be embarrassed because sometimes that was the way the body responded to pain. That didn't seem to make him any less embarrassed. We changed the subject and tried to keep him distracted. It sort of worked. We think he was most frustrated that he couldn't control his limbs. We told him his body was really excited that it was going to bald, and the shaking was the body's way of responding to that excitement. Although it was a crock of shit, we were determined to make him feel as comfortable as possible. He appreciated the attempts at logic, and we finished as quickly as possible. To us, that's a silly thing to be embarrassed about. It wasn't anything he could control.

Adrenaline can also make clients nauseous. A man came in for a back and chest wax before his honeymoon. It's a lot of surface area to cover for a first timer, but it was a special occasion. He handled the back pretty well, but he got pale when ME waxed his chest.

The next time he came in, he only got his back done. He said the chest wax made him too sick to his stomach, and it took awhile for that to pass, so he didn't think it was worth it.

It has been so much fun having men of all ages come to the salon to get services done. It's so different than waxing chicks all day long.

One day, ME waxed a guy in his mid-twenties who had dark hair that was pretty stubborn to remove. At the time, she thought he handled the service well because we laughed our asses off throughout the whole thing. About six weeks later, he came back. She was psyched to see him again, because he was a really nice guy and fun to do. OK, that didn't sound right...

She told him that she was happy he decided to come back and get it done again. She assumed he was getting a Brazilian done because that was what he got the previous time he came to the salon. When he walked into the room, he started to undress, so what would you think he was having done? ME made some kind of comment about this being the second time he was getting waxed and how it much easier it would be this time around.

That's when he told her, "Step back and relax." For the record, he was the one who stepped back with both hands in front of him in the stop position. He said that getting a Brazilian was too fucking painful, and he didn't think he'd ever do it again. However, getting his crack to sac waxed was one of the most rewarding things he had ever done in his life.

Having people say things like that is pretty rewarding to ME as well. She couldn't argue with him that the Brazilian had to be painful for him. That was fine. She gave him a thorough sac-to-crack wax and sent him on his way. Now that is definitely something you don't hear every day.

ME thoroughly understands how important the penis is to a man. She wants to reassure all her male clients that she does her best to treat each appendage with the utmost care and respect. The service will in no way injure your ability to function like a stallion. It just may be a bit tender for a hot minute. And it will feel hot, believe me. In addition, the service should not emasculate you in any way, shape, or form when your penis takes on the shape of a little cigar nub. Please remember that she is a professional who is performing a service that countless men partake in. The size, shape, or girth of your penis is non-consequential to her. She just wants to clean up your parts and make them as smooth and sexy as possible, just like she enjoys doing for women.

ME wants to add that she doesn't think your jewels should hide knee-deep in sea grass and is thrilled when you muster the courage to do something about it. She applauds your willingness to alter the natural state of disarray that can encompass your favorite body part. Believe me, the value of your jewels exponentially increases when she can actually find them.

During an appointment, an older man confided to ME that he was a cross-dresser. She's worked on a lot of cross-dressers in her career, so his confession was not shocking in the least. During her career, she has done hair, nails, makeup, and waxing on men who enjoy dressing like women. That kind of information doesn't affect how she approaches the service or the client. It's simply a statement of fact.

This particular client said that it was difficult wearing women's clothing because he had so much hair on his body. Now that was a fact ME was interested in and knew she could help with. Furthermore, he said that shaving his entire body was a total bitch, but he didn't have much choice. He was a really hairy guy, and it hard looking like a woman with so much hair sticking out of his clothing. She told him that she'd love to wax his chest and back. That was hard for him to do, however, because he hated letting it grow out.

He told her that his long-term partner died of cancer and he was sad and lonely, which was apparent. He said that it really hard to find men to date at this particular juncture in his life. They had a great talk, and she hoped she did her part to make him feel better.

Their exchange got her thinking. She kind of wished she could set up a dating service, because she meets so many people who are lonely. She's been blessed to be happy with the same man for many years, but that isn't the norm these days. If something happens to Mark, how will ME find someone else? She's not sure where she'd start looking. She got to thinking about starting her own dating site. Then she thought about what she would call it. Here's what she came up with: What do you think of Let ME Bond the Bald? (for my friends and followers who believe that sex is better when you wax it all). Or maybe Hooking Up the Hair-Free and Horny (a more Grinder type of site)? What about Smooth and Sexy Singles Seek Somebody? Last, but not least: Luscious Ladies Seeking Groomed Gentlemen. Oh, we could go on forever with this line of thinking!

As Mark's and ME's children have gotten older, it's common for their friends to come into the salon. Most of them are girls, but every once in a while one of their guy friends come in. One of Mark's and ME's daughter's friends came in after a big waxing discussion the night before at a local bar. One friend talked about how much he loved getting his back waxed at the salon. As the drinking continued, so did the bravado of the fellows in the crowd. Next thing you know, two of the guys made appointments to come get waxed. One wanted a Brazilian and the other wanted a back wax.

It was obvious that the guy who came in for the Brazilian was nervous. He was a big, strong college athlete who we expected would put on a tough act. That wasn't the case. His sensitive skin and coarse hair made his Brazilian a painful experience. When he first got on the table, he told ME that he was worried about getting an erection. After a few minutes into the service, he screamed, "I have never been so soft in my entire life!" It was hard to feel any sympathy for him because his friend and I were laughing so hard. Yes, he had a friend in the room for moral support.

As it turns out, his friend was no help at all. All he was interested in doing was recording the experience on his phone and laughing at him. At one point, the guy asked for something to bite on. All we could think to give him was one of the Popsicle sticks. By the time we finished, the Popsicle stick was destroyed. While ME was giving him the Brazilian, his other friend was getting his back waxed by one of her staff members in another room. The guy taking the videos went back and forth checking in on his buddies. He told our "soft guy" that their friend was doing great in the other room. He was just lying there, not making any noise. Meanwhile, our guy was yelling at the top of his lungs, sweating profusely, and squirming all over the table. When he heard how good his friend was dealing with his back wax, he yelled, "This is the first time in my entire life that I wish I had back hair!"

When ME finished waxing him, she went into the hallway, and one of her regulars was waiting for her. She was sitting there with a funny smile on her face. She could hear everything the guy had been yelling and found it funny as well. It may sound sadistic, but it's impossible not to laugh sometimes when you hear someone screaming.

ME thanked her client for waiting and escorted her into a different room. The client stood up to follow ME into the other room, and the first thing she said was, "So, how soft was he?"

ME started laughing and said, "Soft. Really soft."

After she finished this client, ME went back into the first room to do the next appointment. When she walked in there, the pillow was on the floor and the bed sheets were all over the place. The client asked what the hell happened in there. ME told her that she had tough time waxing a her daughter's friend.

The client said it looked like we were wrestling. Yep, ME assured her that they were. As she put on her gloves, the client asked what was on the floor. ME walked around the table and and looked on the floor, and it was the Popsicle stick he was chewing on. She picked it up. It was so gross. It was soaking wet, a little shredded, and had visible teeth marks on it. Both women started laughing hard and the client said, "Men are such babies!" Yes, sometimes they are.

We've talked about erections. We've talked about the penis trying to hide in the abyss. So have you figured out why this chapter is called "Jack-in-the-Box?" We'd like to introduce you to our friend Harry. Remember, the name is fictitious to protect the innocent (and sometimes the guilty). No matter how well he copes with the service, he won't be hairy when he leaves the salon, in case you were wondering. This is Harry's story.

Whenever we touch any part of Harry's private area, his penis moves. And by moves, we mean grows. But as soon as we wax off a section of hair, it shrinks right up. Throughout every Brazilian we've done on him, his penis acts like an accordion. Big, small, big, small. You get the picture. We don't give it the chance to get that big, because we work so fast that it is constantly retracting. You can almost hear an accordion-like sound emanating from his midsection. We wish there was a way that we could mimic the sound we hear in our head every time we wax him. It's almost like a saw going back and forth through a piece of wood. Wood. Get it? Good one.

You'd think that this encounter would be awkward, but it isn't. You see, the first time he came in, the same thing happened. As soon as ME touched him, it started to grow. He apologized to her right up front because he was afraid that his member wasn't behaving. She told him it was fine. He said that he didn't have any control over it. She gets that. The fact that he put it on the table took all of the weirdness away. She appreciated that, and unlike the "erection guy," he said something about it instead of pretending it wasn't happening.

His ever-so-active ping-pongy penis that goes back and forth between happy and sad reminds us of a young child's first encounter with a jack-in-the-box. The hand on the Popsicle stick is like a child's hand on the lever of the toy, and that is what allows Jack to go in and out. If you take that thinking to the next level, like a perverted dude might, you will probably agree with me that Jack's goal in life is to get in the proverbial box.

BOING!
Robbins 2015

The Pussy Prophet

Through ME's years doing Brazilians, she feels she has gained knowledge in so many different areas. She knows a lot about the work that goes into not only in running a salon, but also what is needed to be proficient in the areas of hair, nails, and esthetics. She's tried to capitalize on the relationships she has developed over the course of her almost thirty-year career at Mark & M. E., because that is what truly has made their business successful. Being good at the job is only half the battle. The relationships you develop with your clients are what make everything worthwhile.

That being said, she'd like to impart some words of wisdom that have meant so much to her over the years. She has no idea where many of these expressions came from, but she liked them and wanted to share them with you. For instance, she totally agreed with a statement she once heard that said, "A bald beaver does to a man what a dangling carrot does to a rabbit." Some may think this is silly. She thinks it's profound. A smooth, bald pussy is the biggest aphrodisiac around.

She tried to give sound advice to a young woman who was moving to Colorado. The girl was terrified about getting a Brazilian from someone else. ME gave her the list of the normal questions she recommends people ask when checking out other waxing salons. Since the woman was going to Colorado where pot is legal, ME gave her an added bit of advice that she thought might be helpful. After going through her checklist, ME told the woman that she hoped the salon gave her a blunt before she got her Brazilian. Even though getting high isn't recommended before a waxing service, it was an apropos suggestion. The girl couldn't stop laughing because she thought it would probably make a potentially shitty service way better.

When ME blogged about the conversation, she learned that many followers didn't know what a blunt was. She expected some readers to question the blog, and they didn't disappoint her. A woman asked her straight up what a blunt was, so ME gave her the definition from the Urban Dictionary. We've had a good time looking up all sorts of funny and disgusting things there. It's an amusing site. In case you are also in the dark about what we're referring to, a blunt is basically a marijuana cigarette. Since the woman was going to Denver where pot is legal, it seemed like a plausible scenario. Get it now?

ME is totally an anti-shave kind of gal. She removes any hair that seems unnecessary on any part of her own body with wax. When customers complain that their skin is all messed up from shaving, especially in the pubic area, it's hard for her to feel sympathetic. She understands that waxing is expensive, but she thinks that having a pretty pussy is worth every penny. When a girl told her that she could play "connect the dots" with the ingrown hairs she got from shaving, ME was glad she had a sense of humor about her ugly bikini line. It was indeed ugly.

Our clients make some profound statements, and we would be remiss if we didn't share some of their brilliance as well. A woman in her mid-twenties brought her sister in to observe the waxing process. Having extra people in the room often leads to more colorful conversation.

As the girl was trying to sell the whole Brazilian concept to her sister, she mentioned the monetary commitment, which is a big part of why so many people avoid getting them. Well, that and the pain, of course. She told her sister that even though she pays sixty dollars for a Brazilian every month, she feels like a million dollars when she leaves the salon. That was music to our ears and a symphony to our soul.

We love when brides come in for what we like to call a "honeymoon wax." Basically, a honeymoon wax refers to a woman who gets a Brazilian before she gets married. It's not any different than a regular Brazilian wax. We generally don't leave hearts on the front of the pubis or the groom's initials. Calling it a honeymoon wax is our reminder to the brides out there that they should get a Brazilian before their nuptials.

It's a lot more fun when the bride brings in her wedding party or friends for this monumental experience. One day, a bachelorette party came to the shop. The girls were there to support the bride when she got her first Brazilian. ME saw two of the girls sitting in the waiting room. She asked them what was going on. They said they were waiting for the bride and another one of their friend's. ME asked them where the champagne was. They didn't realize we allowed champagne at the salon. We told them where the closest liquor store was, and they went out to buy splits of champagne.

Once everyone was assembled, we went upstairs to our largest room. The girls circled around the bride's head while we started to perform the service on her. One woman commented that she was a lesbian and went to sit down in the corner. She was the only one who was unable to watch her friend get the Brazilian. ME didn't understand why the woman couldn't watch since she was an actual fan of that particular body part, so she asked her what the deal was. The woman said that she couldn't handle watching anyone hurt a pussy *because* she was so fond of it. That was logic we could understand.

The next thing you know, they were taking a lot of pictures of the bride's expressions. They made sure they all had their thumbs up in positive acknowledgment of this new and exciting thing that was happening to their girlfriend. It truly was a Kodak moment.

We love it when brides get waxed before their honeymoons, because sex can be really uncomfortable when they shave. Hair bumps, razor burn, and stubble can make a person miserable. The negative effects of shaving are nothing new or monumental. Most of us have experienced the irritation that shaving such a sensitive area can cause. We want our brides to avoid such misery between their legs. When a woman is toying with the idea of whether or not she should get a wax before their big day, we suggest that she rubs some sandpaper on her face and between her legs, and the decision will be made for her. You may find yourself thinking twice before butchering your bush with the dreaded Bic. By the way, we vehemently believe that your wedding night shouldn't be the only time you splurge for a wax.

In our opinion, if we are going to wax off all of your pubic hair, then we must include all the hair on the lower part of your stomach. We always ask permission before we wax a woman's happy trail, which is that particular strip of hair that travels from the belly button to the bikini line. One woman referred to that area as her treasure trail, not her happy trail. There was a possibility that she may have had hidden treasures in the thick mound of hair that covered that particular part of her body. It was no treasure. It was a travesty.

Men can also say wise and clever things when we are talking about waxing. This cute, young guy who came in for his second wax told ME straight out that getting a Brazilian was life changing. She can live with that mantra. We have heard similar confessions from women, but it was cool coming from a guy. We completely, 100 percent agree that waxing off your pubic hair can be life changing, and it's awesome to know that we are not alone in this conviction.

Amid the rampant sex talk that happens on a daily basis at the salon comes more brilliance that we must share with you. ME was having a conversation about orgasms with a girl. You really thought that was a taboo topic? Think again, my friends. I can't remember exactly what they were talking about, but she suddenly commented that it pissed her off that guys can get off just by sticking their cocks in pudding, whereas chicks are way more complicated and take more effort to get off. I can't say that I ever imagined having sex with tapioca, but I totally understood the point she was trying to make. Guys do have it much easier. Women have brains and emotions and other shit that get in the way sometimes. It's just how they're wired.

Dudes Got It Easy

It's so much easier
For dudes to get off;
Just a little rub
Or just a little cough

Will make it get hard.
It happens so fast!
They don't care
How long it will last.

If there's a hole
Anywhere around,
Don't be surprised
If you hear a moaning sound.

Girls have it harder.
It takes more work
To make it happen.
Don't give me that smirk.

We wish we could cum
As easy as you,
We need more than a tug
Or a tight little shoe.

We need our brains
To connect with your cock,
Or the puss just won't work,
The feeling will block.

You could stick it in pudding
And love every minute,
Your bodies work so well
As long as you're in it.

So maybe we're jealous,
Just a tidbit,
But we still are in love
With our cute little clit.

And we have something
Over you:
We can cum more than once,
And we often do.

More Random Shit People Tell Me

The first chapter that ME ever wrote was in her first book (*The Happy Hoo-Ha*), and it was called "Crazy Shit People Tell Me." She decided it was only fitting that she write about more crazy shit that people shared to end this happy trail of humor that she embarked on so many years ago.

Chicks have hair in the crack of their asses just like guys do. We don't make a big deal about it. We just get rid of it, because it's gross. Many women refer to it as their tails. It often looks like a tail, so that it is a perfectly sound description. But this discussion is actually about ME's car. Didn't see that coming, did you?

One day a woman came in with her hands on her hips and a disapproving smile. She was upset about ME's license plate. She is a woman in her forties who had been coming to Mark & M. E. for years. The personalized license plate reads, "Wax It All." However, there are no spaces in between the words on the actual plate. For as long as ME has had this license plate, which was from 2011, this particular client thought the plate read, "Wax Tail."

This client is a licensed cosmetologist who has been following ME's writing for years. She learned what the license plate said in the second book and was upset that she read it wrong all these years. Not only did she think the license plate said, "Wax Tail," she was convinced that she saw the words "wax tail" every time she came to the salon for a wax.

Unfortunately, she didn't have the name right. But it didn't matter, because we do wax the tails of women all day long. She was disgruntled, because she felt stupid for not understanding what the license plate actually said. No big deal. It was a strange thing to be upset about, but that's OK. Wax tail is pretty funny.

ME often wears a baseball cap with the words, "Mark & M. E. Wax Queen" on it. One day at the supermarket, the man cashing her out asked her if she was the ME at Mark & M. E. His ex-girlfriend had been a regular client at Mark & M. E. for years. He spoke highly of her and said that they still talked once in a while.

Shortly thereafter, we received a Facebook message from the client. We told her that we met her ex and that he was nice. She told ME that she should have told him that she had a longer standing relationship with her pussy than he did. You have to admit that line is classic, and ME wished she had been feeling wittier that day and said something that clever.

When pubic hair is dense and curly, it's easier to form shapes into it. When white girls with thin, stringy pubes want us to put cute shapes or their man's initials in that area, it just isn't happening. One afternoon, a black lady came in with an impressive Afro between her legs. She started out the conversation by saying that she was tempted to use a straight edge to groom it because there was so much there to work with. And she wasn't kidding.

We could have done a variety of shapes or letters in her mound. It was the perfect landscape. But she said that all she was interested in was a Brazilian buzz cut. And that was exactly what she got. We did the army proud.

Women really do say some funny shit. One woman told us that she had a really furry bunny between her legs. If we used our imaginations, we could say that her hair indeed looked like a furry bunny. She continued this thought by saying that it was a shame it wasn't Easter, because it would make her ability to grow a bunny between her legs even funnier. It wasn't even remotely near Easter. Easter or not, we were up for the challenge of skinning that rabbit. Once the bunny was skinned, ME told her it was safe to use her electronic rabbit without her hair getting tangled in it. Safety comes first, you know.

It's tough to come in for a wax on a regular basis when you have small children at home. There are those times, however, when your children say things that make you want to run to the salon for a wax at a warped speed.

For example, one of our relatively new moms was taking a bath with her two-year-old daughter. She is a white woman with very dark hair. The little girl wanted to know why her mommy had a "black bagina." Well, if that doesn't make you want to come see us, I don't know what does.

It is almost impossible not to remember your first-ever Brazilian bikini wax. ME has waxed some women for nearly twenty years. Women remind her on a regular basis how many years she has waxed them. When clients tells her that she has waxed them for five, ten, or even fifteen years, she is always amazed at how much time has passed.

One day, this young woman wished her an enthusiastic happy anniversary. ME had started waxing this client for her wedding, and she was celebrating her one-year anniversary. ME loves that she was part of that special day. Not only did the client wish her a happy anniversary, she gave her a big hug. It was a hug that was naked from the waist down, but it was a hug none the less. Who said ripping hair out of women's crotches can't be rewarding?

When pubic hair is sitting on a wax strip, it looks like all sorts of things. The roots and the hair are kind of cool to look at, but, for the most part, it's pretty gross. If we had to say what the hair most looks like on the strip, we would say it resembles a dead animal. A woman told me that one of the strips with her hair on it looked like a dead rodent. That analogy has always been spot on. Another woman said it looked like a caterpillar. We always thought caterpillars were kind of cute, but we're not sure we think they're cute anymore. It's funny how your job can distort your perception of the world.

Do people say crazy shit in the confines of the wax rooms? They sure do. It's all those crazy things that gave us enough material to write three books on Brazilian bikini waxing. Mark thought ME was crazy when she said she was writing a third book, but she had so much material that she wanted to share that she couldn't stop with two. Thank you for all of the crazy shit you have said to her and done to her over the years. It has made her career more worthwhile than you could ever imagine.

Reflections of ME

Hey, it's ME again. At this particular moment, I'm sitting on the deck of a condo that my mom owns in the Florida Keys, just staring at the ocean. I do this for hours at a time when I am here. And, believe me, I try to come down here as much as possible during the winter. Rochester, New York, leaves a lot to be desired between the months of November and April. I absolutely love the Florida Keys. It's my favorite place to go on vacation. I started coming to the Keys when I was about ten years old, and, for some reason, I can never seem to get my fill.

Countless memories surround me as I sit here feeling reflective and nostalgic. I have memories of vacationing here with my parents, siblings, and grandfather every Christmas and Easter for as long as I can remember. I have a brother and a sister who are a lot older than me, so I didn't vacation here very much with them when I was younger. My other sister Robin and I were the two children in my immediate family fortunate enough to come with our mom and dad on a regular basis. I cherish the memories of those vacations.

One time, my mom said we needed to clean the refrigerator out because we were leaving the next day to go back to Buffalo (which is where I was raised). We had a storage unit attached to our condo, so certain things could be left in there that wouldn't go bad. I imagine I was only a tween at the time, and Robin is six years older than I am. We proceeded to drink a ton of my dad's Carlo Rossi Burgundy wine, which he always bought by the gallon. I don't think we made a dent in the actually food that was in the fridge, but we knocked out a shit ton of wine. When our parents walked into the condo and saw our drunk asses laughing hysterically in the living room, they tried to be mad. Yeah, the wine could have been put in storage, but that never occurred to us. I don't think we got in trouble though. I think they responded with the whole shaking-of-the-head thing and dismissing our adolescent behavior as amusing.

I remember Robin trying to justify our actions by reminding them that they wanted us to finish off all of the food and drinks in the fridge. I also know that our mom said the wine would have kept. Now that I'm a drinker, I'm not sure how true that statement was. I just remember being the kind of trashed that made us laugh incessantly. You know, the kind of laughing that makes you snort and causes snot to run out of your nose. More than anything, I remember the laughter from that day. I am happy to say that once my folks discovered the Keys, it became our home away from home.

When my sister went off to college, my grandmother passed away, so my grandfather started coming here with us. I have incredible memories of vacationing with him. He was born in 1898 and lived until he was eighty-seven years old. He was a pathologist at Roswell Park in Buffalo, a history and boxing aficionado, and a really special person in my life. I was sad when he passed, but, ironically, it was the same month that I met Mark. I think Grandpa Burke had something to do with that.

My grandparents used to drive to Florida every year once my grandpa retired. My grandfather had never flown on a plane. My grandmother never wanted to. After my grandma died, we brought him to the Keys. He was eighty years old and had never flown on an airplane before. He was born before electricity and planes, so you can only imagine what a thrill it was to fly.

I remember how excited he got when we took off. I was sitting next to him, holding his hand during the takeoff. He loved the feeling of the power of the plane as it took off. To this day, I often still think of him when I fly.

I'll never forget the first time I brought Mark to the Keys. I was overweight when we met, and, even though I had lost most of my excess weight by the time we went on our first vacation together, I was nervous about him seeing me in a bathing suit. Now that I think about it, it really didn't make any sense and just reiterates how whacked-out chicks can be. Not only had we been sleeping together for months, we were unofficially living together. So it's not like he hadn't seen what I looked like without clothes on.

At the time, I had my own apartment to store my shit in, but I slept at his place every night. But there was something about him seeing me in a bathing suit in the bright sunlight that freaked me out. It was terrifying.

Now that years have passed and I look back to that August in 1985, I know it was more than being in the bright sunlight in a bathing suit that made me nervous. I loved our place in the Keys and was so worried that he wouldn't love it as much as I did. After almost a year of dating, I felt pretty committed to this guy and was petrified he wouldn't like my favorite place in the whole world. To top things off, we were going down in the summer, which is a stupid hot month to be traveling to the southernmost tip of the continental United States.

Fortunately, Mark has always liked oppressive heat and loved that it was too hot to just sit on the beach in the sun. We had to put our chairs in the ocean in order to be able to hang outside. The condo is beautiful and the view is breathtaking, but that didn't mean he'd get as excited about it as I did every time I came here. The stars were definitely in our favor, because he felt the connection just as strongly. I guess that must be why I fell in love with a Pisces.

After that trip, we scheduled to travel to the Keys a couple times each year. Ironically, we always came down at the same time as my parents did. They became our travel companions. The month before we got married, we went to the Keys with my folks for the Christmas and New Year holiday.

Although Mark and I didn't have a long engagement, the whole wedding process was stressful. It's incredible how two people and their respective families can find so much bullshit to argue about. While we were here during that holiday, which was less than two months before the actual wedding date, Mark begged me to elope. He wanted to get married on the beach, with just my mom and dad there. I'll never forget when he said that they were our best friends and the most important people to have with us. After nine months of planning, however, I just couldn't do it. I didn't want to ever have regrets about not getting married in a church. Besides, I always worried that his Italian, Catholic mother would resent me for not going through with the wedding we had planned. It was her first son of five to get married, and she was really excited about it. Since she liked me, I didn't want to jeopardize that relationship.

We got married on Valentine's Day in 1987. It was the coldest day of the year, but it was one of the sunniest as well. That night, there was a huge snowstorm, and a lot of the guests had to find rooms at the Marriott where the reception took place, because it was too dangerous to drive. The reception ended up being a cluster-fuck of one mess-up after another. Although the guests had a blast, so many things went wrong that it was really stressful for us. In fact, it kind of sucked. The good news is that there was an open bar the entire night and the 327 people at our wedding had a good time.

Let me give you an idea of what went wrong. The room was supposed to be ready at six o'clock. It was ready at seven, although they didn't bother to vacuum from the earlier party. They were supposed to have four open bars all night. They had two. They didn't have enough seats. They ran out of food. The dance floor kept falling apart while people were dancing, so some guy kept crawling around trying to duct-tape the seams. Needless to say, the majority of the managerial staff was fired after that night. More importantly, we got the majority of our money back. And, even more important than that, is that fact that we are still happily married.

As I continue to sit on the deck, I am watching the boats pass by, and I can't help but remember my dad. In April 1989, Mark and my dad went deep-sea fishing for sharks. It had been Mark's dream for as long as I could remember to catch a big shark. During one our vacations, he did just that. He caught a huge Mako shark that now resides in our family room in Rochester that I mentioned earlier.

A friend of my father's and his son-in-law also went along for the hunt. Fortunately, Mark was the one who snagged the shark. There were no portable cell phones or digital recording devices like we have now, so we were lucky that the son-in-law had a video recorder to record that day. We had such a party when they finally got back to shore. I can't even remember how many pitchers of rumrunners we went through. It was such a happy day, and I was so excited that my husband and father were able to share that experience. It was a Monday.

The next day, Mark and I had to go back to Rochester. We were hanging on the beach in the morning, and Mark offered to help my dad put his sailboat away, since my parents were leaving later in the week. My dad told Mark that he wanted one last sail. That was Tuesday.

The next day, my dad was electrocuted putting his sailboat away. He didn't survive the accident.

The day after my dad died, our son Adryan was born. This was the second time I had lost someone incredibly important to me and another special person was brought into my life. First, I found Mark, and then I had Adryan. This is where my faith lies—in family and in love.

Since then, my sister Gail and I started a tradition where we bring our children to the Keys every Christmas. We both have three children each who love the Keys as much as we do. We have been coming down here together for as long as I can remember, and the memories just keep forming. Two of her boys are married with children. Our kids are currently college age and beyond. When we are down here, we play family games and have beer-pong tournaments every New Years. My kids feel such an intense connection to the Keys, they have tattooed the coordinates of Key Colony Beach on their bodies as a constant reminder of how special this place is. In fact, since I wrote this chapter, I also have a tattoo of the coordinates on my body as well, underneath a tattoo of three palm trees, of course.

I think it must be pretty obvious why I was feeling reflective. The sound of the surf and the warmth of the sun are intoxicating, and I am sitting in a place that is full of all sorts of memories for me. As my reflection continues, I started to think about where I was at this juncture in my life. I just started to seriously laugh out loud.

I wax pussies for a living! Now, if that isn't comical, I don't know what is. I was brought up believing that hard work and happiness were the keys to a fulfilling life. But who the fuck would have ever imagined that waxing vaginas for a living would be so rewarding? My father passed away when I was a schoolteacher and never knew that I joined Mark in the family business. Since he and my mom had a family business, I know it would have made him happy. In addition, I truly believe that he would have gotten the biggest kick out of what I do. You have to admit that it's pretty amusing.

So this is my trail, or my path, and it has truly been a happy one so far. There have been some sad and shitty things in my life too, but that's what it's all about. Yes, a trail in my life can most definitely refer to the strip of hair that starts at your belly button and leads all the way to that special place between your legs. But it means so much more to me. I've waxed thousands of women in my career and left thousands of landing strips (or trails) leading to the promised land. That was my goal and what I got paid to do. I know I have made most of those women happy (after a tiny bit of discomfort, of course.) It has been my personal trail that has been the most interesting.

Even if I never imagined myself doing this kind of work for a living, I knew I'd find something that I could be passionate about doing as a career. I never thought pussies would be the source of that passion, but why not? Everyone wants a happy hoo-ha. Everyone desires a happy hen house and hopes that it is truly the place where someone's cock wants to go. (If you're into cocks, that is.) Most importantly, each one of us should strive to lead our lives *and* our genitals through a journey that follows a happy trail.

Ode To The Pussy

Adam and Eve were the first known lovers;
The lived in the Garden of Eden
Alone with no others
It was hard not to want to love with their bodies,
Since they were alone, naked, and total hotties.

It's hard to believe that a red piece of fruit
Was all it took Adam to indulge in such a beaut.
There was no TV to keep them amused,
So I understand why they'd want their bodies fused.

You have to remember that Eve had a pussy:
It had to be ripe, even if it was bushy.
It would be hard for any man to resist
A tight little pussy and a nice set of tits.

Don't blame Eve for being a woman
Or even Adam for being a human.
Men are controlled by the pussy, that's a fact.
Desire won him over, and that is that.

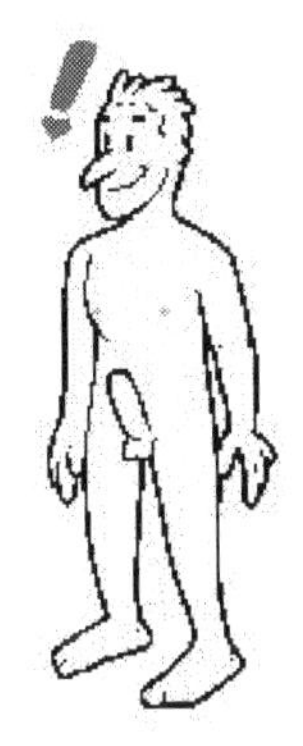

Everyone knows that pussies have control
Over men and their actions and their beings as a whole.
Let's not be eager to assign any blame
Uniting a cock and a cunt is the most pleasurable game.

Men have no control when the pussy is around:
That's why it's so hard to not make any sound.
And how can it be bad when it feels so good?
It's hard to believe that you think that it would.

And if Adam hadn't popped Eve's ripened pink cherry
There'd never be a virgin mother named Mary.
And life as we know it would never exist
Which is why we should celebrate the pussy and a nice set of tits.

Made in the USA
Charleston, SC
23 October 2015